INTERNATI
SOCIALISI
A quarterly journal of socialist theory

Spring 1998
Contents

Editorial

Colin Sparks	*The eye of the storm*	*3*
Shin Gyoung-hee	*The crisis and workers' movement in South Korea*	*39*
Rob Hoveman	*Financial crises and the real economy*	*55*
Peter Morgan	*Class divisions in the gay community*	*77*
Alex Callinicos	*The secret of the dialectic*	*93*
John Parrington	*It's life Jim, but not as we know it*	*105*
Judy Cox	*Robin Hood: earl, outlaw or rebel?*	*119*
Ian Birchall	*The vice-like hold of nationalism? A comment on Megan Trudell's 'Prelude to revolution'*	*133*
William Keach	*In perspective: Alexander Cockburn and Christopher Hitchens*	*143*

Issue 78 of INTERNATIONAL SOCIALISM, quarterly journal of the Socialist Workers Party (Britain)

Published March 1998
Copyright © International Socialism
Distribution/subscriptions: International Socialism,
PO Box 82, London E3.
American distribution: B de Boer, 113 East Center St, Nutley,
New Jersey 07110.
Subscriptions and back copies: PO Box 16085, Chicago
Illinois 60616
Editorial and production: 0171-538 1626/071-538 0538
Sales and subscriptions: 0171-538 5821
American sales: 773 665 7337

ISBN I 898876 37 1

Printed by BPC Wheatons Ltd, Exeter, England
Typeset by East End Offset, London E3
Cover by Sherborne Design Ltd

For details of back copies see the end pages of this book

Subscription rates for one year (four issues) are:

Britain and overseas (surface):	individual	£14.00 ($30)
	institutional	£25.00
Air speeded supplement:	North America	£3.00
	Europe/South America	£3.00
	elsewhere	£4.00

Note to contributors
The deadline for articles intended for issue 80 of
International Socialism is 1 April 1998

All contributions should be double-spaced with wide margins.
Please submit two copies. If you write your contribution
using a computer, please also supply a disk, together with
details of the computer and programme used.

A quarterly journal of socialist theory

THE TIGER economies of South and East Asia were being held up only yesterday as models for success, not least by Tony Blair. But the crash of 1997, whose effects are still unravelling across the industrialised world, put an end to such easy propaganda. In three linked articles we look at the causes and consequences of the crisis. Colin Sparks explains the rise of the Tiger economies and charts the forces that brought them to their knees. Shin Gyoung-hee writes from South Korea on the crisis of profitability which underlay that crash and on the prospects for the region's most militant and combative workers' movement. Rob Hoveman concludes with a restatement of the Marxist account of how financial crashes and industrial slumps are linked, taking his example from the fate of the Tiger economies.

GAY POLITICS are at a crossroads. The celebration of the 'pink economy' which seemed so dominant in the 1980s has increasingly turned sour for many gays and lesbians. The annual Pride march is now in danger of splitting in two, as many react against the commercialism and depoliticisation which has accompanied increasing sponsorship by gay businesses. Peter Morgan examines the class divide among gays and lesbians and traces the ways in which it expresses itself in the debate about the future of the movement.

ALEX CALLINICOS'S article 'The Secret of the Dialectic' reviews a newly published account of Marxist philosophy, *The Algebra of Revolution* by John Rees. John Parrington also looks at dialectics in his review of Steven Rose's new book *Lifelines*. The enduring popularity of the Robin Hood legend is uncovered by Judy Cox in her overview of the history of the myth, from its origins to the present day.

THE RETURN of our occasional 'In Perspective' feature gives William Keach the chance to dissect the work of two radical journalists, Christopher Hitchens and Alex Cockburn.

Editor: John Rees. Assistant editors: Alex Callinicos, Chris Harman, John Molyneux, Lindsey German, Colin Sparks, Mike Gonzalez, Peter Morgan, Mike Haynes, Judy Cox, Megan Trudell, Mark O'Brien and Rob Hoveman.

The eye of the storm

COLIN SPARKS

It seems only yesterday that the South and East Asian 'Tiger' economies were being held up as models of problem-free capitalist expansion. But now currencies collapse, stock markets tumble and banks close. Huge industrial conglomerates go bankrupt. Politicians dither and totter. Teams from the IMF fly in to dictate the terms for a bail out. Even in Japan the economy remains stalled on the brink of a major recession, while the long trail of financial scandals runs on and on. At the end of January the finance minister was forced to resign after police raided his ministry and arrested two officials on suspicion of taking bribes to reveal commercial secrets.[1] Even the resources of what is easily the largest and most established economy in the region, indeed the second largest economy in the world, seem insufficient to resolve the crisis.

Yet the Tigers were supposed to be examples of a new phase of capitalist development. Their phenomenal rates of growth demonstrated that capitalism was still an enormously vigorous and expansionary system. The scale and continuity of their growth demonstrated that there was a way around the cycle of boom and slump that socialist critics have always claimed to be endemic to capitalism. Their social peace demonstrated that the idea that class struggle is the inevitable accompaniment of class society was the product of Marxist imaginations. The very achievements of their young people in literacy and numeracy demonstrated both the inadequacies of trendy 'red teachers' and the degeneracy of Western (male) youth. Travelling through the region from the banks

and factories of Seoul to the nascent 'multimedia super-corridor' outside
Kuala Lumpur, wide eyed Western commentators like Martin Jacques,
the former editor of *Marxism Today*, found the living embodiment of the
gleaming, problem-free New Times that they believed had replaced
socialism as the alternative future of humanity. In a typically lyrical
passage the World Bank *Annual Report 1997* said:

> *East Asia's capacity to sustain rapid growth is without precedent. The only
> significant group of countries to close the gap with the industrialised
> economies over the past few decades, their growth has averaged 7 percent
> per year in real terms since the mid-1970s, accelerating to 9 percent per year
> in the 1990s. China's growth has been astonishing, with per capita income
> rising 270 percent in 17 years... East Asia enjoys enviable macroeconomic
> conditions and an unprecedented growth momentum...*[2]

To be fair, the bank did identify one or two problems that needed tin-
kering with, but it was convinced that 'the prospects for continued high
growth in coming years remain sound.' Even without the benefit of hind-
sight, this passage surely has the selfsame congratulatory and uncritical
tone as some Stalinist acolyte of the 1930s praising the achievements of
the latest Five Year Plan.

Now, in one of those extraordinary ideological transformations at
which bourgeois thinkers are so adept, there is general rejoicing that
crony capitalism has had its comeuppance. All of the shortcomings manifested by societies which have developed with extreme rapidity from
subsistence agriculture to industrial capitalism have come to light. The
rotten foundations of the banking system have been exposed. The
grandiose projects to acquire the trappings of an advanced industrial
economy, like the Indonesian plan to build an aerospace industry, have
been revealed as ludicrous fantasies on the part of corrupt politicians and
their profiteering friends and relations. The solution to the world's problems is no longer to make the West more like the East, but to make the
East more like the West. A particularly unpleasant example of this sort of
attitude was provided by one Jeffrey Bartholet, who found it impossible
to decide whether he wanted to adopt a patronising sneer or just indulge
in some good old fashioned gloating when he wrote:

> *Can South Korea become an open, Western-style economy? To an extent, it
> has to. The IMF demanded that Seoul open Korean companies to foreign
> ownership. Already, the government is allowing non-hostile takeovers—a
> shock in a nation where most companies are so tightly held they rarely
> welcome fellow Koreans as partners. But Koreans now have little choice but
> to sell to foreigners...Western companies...often open internal accounts to*

*their private bankers. But South Korean conglomerates never have, and are
sure to balk at foreign investors who demand to see their books. 'Those
accounts are the source of dirty funds,' says* [one] *banker. 'Making payments
to ghost people and returning the money to the company coffers was the way
they got money to bribe government officials. So they had to keep those
accounts in their own hands. In Asia, the emperor comes first and after him
the rule of law'... A habit of greasing palms runs deep in South Korea...*[3]

The IMF, as the chosen instrument of the international ruling class,
will sort out the web of protectionist and anti-competitive policies that
have given these economies an unfair advantage in international trade.[4]
There may be unexpected shocks, there will certainly be far too many red
figures in the balance sheets, and there is always a danger that something
really nasty will happen in Japan, but on balance it looks to the bourgeoisie as though the worst is over. Slimmed down, tamed, reformed,
transparent, and deeply in hock to Western governments and banks, the
chastened former Tigers will in the future be much more dependable, and
much more junior, partners in a new phase of capitalist growth.

Most of the explanations offered in the West for all of this by bourgeois commentators are, frankly, racist. Such writers assume that 'they',
the Asians, are fundamentally different from 'us', the Westeners. These
differences explain their economic success. We are idle and enjoy only
our leisure. They are industrious and love hard work. We like to spend
our wages without thought of the morrow. They prefer to save for a rainy
day. We are obstinately attached to things like independent working class
organisations and democratic practices that get in the way of economic
efficiency. They know better, and like nothing more than a strong
paternal hand, whether from the leader of the country or the boss of the
company. A similar set of fundamental characteristics is invoked to
explain the recent economic catastrophes. We run open and transparent
businesses. They prefer secrecy. We have contractual relationships. They
do favours for their chums. We know how to close unsuccessful companies. They do not. We understand that business is about profit. They
mistakenly believe market share is important. The fact that these myths
are equally assiduously propagated by the local apologists for the ruling
classes of South and East Asia does not make them any less unpleasant.

As well as exposing this rubbish, there are serious problems for Marxists
to address. It is one thing to ridicule bourgeois myths for the ludicrous nonsense that they are, but it is another, and very much more important, task to
discover whether there is some special kind of capitalism that has different
dynamics to those of the familiar 'Western' model. We need to understand
why these economies were able to grow so fast, and why that growth
reached the limits it did. We need to be able to explain why the crisis has
taken place, and why it took place just when it did and just in the form that

it did. We need to have some sense of the ways in which the crisis is affecting the working class in those countries, and what the prospects are for them to resist the sacrifices they are being asked to endure. The present article is more concerned with the background to the recent events, and analyses the patterns of growth and stagnation in the region as a whole.

The myth of 'Asian values'

The first myth that needs exploding is that we are discussing a homogenous and uniform region. First the boom and then the bust have been attributed to some set of Asian values that all of the countries in the region share. There are certainly similarities between the countries of the region, in the same way as there are similarities between the countries of Europe. There are, for example, some quite strong similarities in the way that their economies are run that we will need to look at in more detail. On the other hand, there are also sharp differences at all levels. Whatever racist Western 'experts' or Eastern apologists for tyranny may claim, there is no single, homogenous 'Asian' set of characteristics that explains what has been going on in the region.

We can demonstrate this by looking at some very obvious facts that ought to be well enough known to everyone who comments on the region. At almost every level there is less evidence of a monolithic 'Asian' unity than there is of an equally mythical 'European' unity. In important aspects of ethnicity, language and culture, South and East Asia are at least as diverse as anywhere else. European religious belief, for example, is primarily Christian, although with important Jewish and Muslim components of very long standing. It would be difficult to make any parallel claim in South and East Asia. To take only the major religions: Malaysia and Indonesia are predominantly Muslim; the Philippines (Catholic) Christian and Muslim; Thailand Bhuddist; China partly Bhuddist, partly Taoist; Japan partly Bhuddist, partly Shintoist; Korea partly Bhuddist, partly (Protestant) Christian; and so on. The idea that a single set of beliefs has permeated the value systems of all these countries and so produced similar economic behaviour is palpable nonsense.

The historical experiences of the countries of the region are different too. Malaysia was the victim of British imperialism, and Hong Kong and Singapore were, of course, actually set up as outposts of that empire. Indonesia was ruled by the Dutch. The Philippines experienced first Spanish and then US colonial rule. Korea, Taiwan and much of China were subjected to Japan, which itself was a minor colonial power up until its defeat by the US in 1945. Thailand, balancing between British and French imperialism, managed to avoid formal subordination to any foreign power. There is no common legacy of the past that can be used to explain the present and future.

On a shorter time scale, and more importantly for our purposes, the timing and speed of capitalist development have varied widely from country to country. Japan began its industrial development after the Meiji restoration in 1868. For a long time it was the only industrial economy in the region. We have looked at its growth in detail in an earlier issue of this journal, and it is quite clear that Japan was a substantial, modern, industrial country by 1970 at the very latest.[5] In the 1970s Singapore, Hong Kong, Taiwan and South Korea began a period of rapid economic growth that led to them being labelled the 'Four Small Tigers'. Subsequently, in the 1980s and 1990s, these countries have been joined by the 'Tiger cubs': China, Malaysia, Thailand and most recently Indonesia, with, possibly, the Philippines as the newest member of the club. These different time scales of development mean that the various countries grew in different phases of the world market, and their economies and social structure have, as Table 1 shows, very different shapes.[6]

TABLE 1: GROSS PRODUCTS OF SELECTED COUNTRIES (1995)

Country	Population (millions)	GDP (US$ million)	GNP per capita (US$)	GNP per capita PPP (US$)
China	1,200.2	687,647	620	2,920
Indonesia	193.3	198,079	980	3,800
Philippines	68.6	74,180	1,050	2,850
Thailand	58.2	167,056	2,740	7,540
Malaysia	20.1	85,311	3,890	9,020
ROC (Taiwan)	21.3	241,000	11,604	—
(South) Korea	44.9	455,476	9,700	11,450
Hong Kong	6.2	143,669	22,990	22,950
Singapore	3.0	83,695	26,730	22,770
Japan	125.2	5,108,540	39,640	22,110
US	263.1	6,952,020	26,980	26,980

[Source: World Bank and ROC]

The first thing that is evident from this table is that the economies we are discussing are of very different sizes. This is a central fact that must be remembered in any discussion of the crisis in Asia. Japan, by far the largest in the group, is a truly colossal economy. It is close, in terms of size and per capita GDP, to the US. At the other end of the scale, Singapore and Hong Kong, although with high per capita GDPs, are tiny in absolute size. Singapore is a city state in fact, and Hong Kong is one in effect. Some of the economies in between are significant, but even the largest, South Korea and mainland China, are of an order of magnitude

smaller than that of Japan. It therefore follows that the impact of any
crisis on the world economy will be far more severe to the extent that it
involves Japan. However serious the South Korean, Thai or Indonesian
crises may be, and however devastating their effects on the lives of the
working class, they do not spell automatic doom for world capitalism.
As we shall see, these crises in the smaller economies could still have
very serious effects around the world, through their ability to affect the
development of the crisis inside Japan itself among other things, but it is
important to keep a sense of proportion with regard to the scale of the
economies currently involved in meltdown.

The second obvious fact that emerges from Table 1 is that these countries are at very different levels of development, as measured in GDP per
capita, either in simple dollar terms or adjusted for the effect of exchange
rate variations (ie the fourth column). In fact, these differences are recognised by the various bodies that attempt to manage international
capitalism. Japan, South Korea, Hong Kong and Singapore are classified
by the World Bank as 'high income economies' (and Japan and South
Korea are members of the OECD). In these terms at least, they are effectively developed, industrialised societies of the kind found in Europe and
North America. Malaysia is 'upper middle income'. Thailand, Indonesia
and the Philippines are 'lower middle income', while China is 'low
income'. This broad group of countries are 'developing' in the same way
as are India, Jamaica, Turkey or Chile, although, as we shall see, their
rates of growth are very high by international standards.

TABLE 2: STRUCTURE OF PRODUCTION IN SELECTED COUNTRIES (1995)

Country	Percentage of labour force in agriculture	Distribution GDP (percent)		
		Agriculture	Industry	Services
China	74	21	48	31
Indonesia	57	17	42	41
Philippines	45	22	32	46
Thailand	64	11	40	49
Malaysia	27	13	43	44
(ROC) Taiwan	—	4	37	59
(South) Korea	18	7	43	50
Hong Kong	1	0	17	83
Singapore	0	0	36	64
Japan	7	2	38	60
Germany	4	1	31	68
US	3	2	26	72

[Source: World Bank, OECD, ROC]

The differences in the economic structures are even clearer when we look at the data in Table 2.[7] Japan, Hong Kong and Singapore are countries in which the transition to an urban capitalist productive structure is more or less complete. South Korea and Taiwan are approaching that position. The other countries of the region retain large or very large agricultural populations engaged in unproductive agriculture. They have substantial urban populations, and within those substantial industrial sectors. These latter are extremely productive in value terms relative to the rest of the economy. These are economies in which the motor of dynamic social development is obviously the same as that which transformed Britain, Belgium and the north eastern US 150 years ago. Factories are being built. Peasants are turning into proletarians in one lifetime. Industrial capitalism is being constructed out of the ruins of earlier modes of production. The more developed economies present a rather more complex picture. In fact, the tiny economy of Hong Kong is even more 'post-industrial' than is the US. In the course of the 1980s the economy of Hong Kong shifted, in value terms, away from indigenous production towards the provision of financial services and acting as an intermediary for the trade into and out of mainland China. Japan and, increasingly, South Korea are, in terms of the structure of advanced economies in the contemporary world, pre-eminently industrial capitalist economies of the classic kind. Their economic structures resemble most closely the massive and highly industrialised German economy. They are countries dominated by big scale modern factories in which the classical industrial proletariat working in manufacturing is the largest social class.

These differences mean that the impact of the economic crisis takes a different form from country to country. In particular, the different levels of economic development affect the kinds of goods and services that the various countries trade on the world market. The smaller and later developing countries tend to have industries that are at a relatively low level of sophistication. A large section of their industrial bases depends on imported specialist items that they then work up and re-export. In contrast, Japan has very sophisticated industries that need to import raw materials but which provide finished and semi-finished manufactured goods for export. Again the later developers are, in general, net recipients of foreign capital, while Japan is the world's largest exporter of capital. A crisis in Thailand or South Korea has an effect on banks in Japan that have loaned heavily to capitalists in these countries. As we shall see, these factors mean that the capitalist class in various countries identifies its majority interests in different ways, making it even more difficult to achieve a resolution to the crisis that satisfies everybody.

Was there an economic miracle?

The short answer is: yes. However unpalatable it may be to would be Marxists who believe that humanity's productive forces can only stagnate and decline, there has in fact been an enormous expansion in the last couple of decades, much of it concentrated in South and East Asia. Not only have these economies changed and grown, but parts of the population have experienced the benefits as well as the hardships that capitalism bestows compared to less productive economic systems.

Table 3 shows the rates of growth for some of the main sectors of the economy since 1980.[8] These show that, while all of the economies in the region grew quickly during the period, there were some striking differences between them. Japan, the most mature of the economies, had experienced its most rapid periods of industrial growth during earlier decades, and this period demonstrated that its pace of growth was slowing down to one closer to the 'high income countries' average (2.0 percent per annum during 1990-1995), and actually falling below that of the US. Of the other major economies, something of a slowdown was also experienced by South Korea, although its rate of growth remained much higher than that of other comparable countries. The less developed countries, on the other hand, experienced high rates of growth during the 1980s, and even higher ones during the 1990s. What is more, the rate of growth of industry, and of the value of goods and services exported, rose more quickly than did overall GDP.

TABLE 3: THE PACE OF CHANGE IN SOUTH AND EAST ASIA

Country	Average annual percentage growth rate					
	GDP		Industry		Exports	
	1980-90	1990-95	1980-90	1990-95	1980-90	1990-95
China	10.2	12.8	11.1	18.1	11.5	15.6
Indonesia	6.1	7.6	6.9	10.1	2.9	10.8
Philippines	1.0	2.3	-0.9	2.2	3.5	9.4
Thailand	7.6	8.4	9.9	10.8	14.0	14.2
Malaysia	5.2	8.7	7.2	11.0	10.9	14.4
(ROC) Taiwan	—	(6.5)	—	—	—	—
(South) Korea	9.4	7.2	13.1	7.3	12.0	13.4
Hong Kong	6.9	5.6	—	—	14.4	13.5
Singapore	6.4	8.7	5.4	9.2	10.0	—
Japan	4.0	1.0	4.2	0.0	4.5	3.4
US	3.0	2.6	2.8	1.2	5.2	7.3

[Source: World Bank, ROC]

Growth of this kind, taking place at such a phenomenally rapid rate, inevitably transforms some parts of society and leaves other parts untouched. Apart from Japan, Hong Kong and Singapore, these countries are all classic examples of what Marxists call 'combined and uneven' development. They exhibit many of the most advanced social features cheek-by-jowl with many of the most backward. From the tops of the huge skyscrapers of Shanghai, one can see villages that have not yet experienced an agricultural revolution. The modern proletarian, working in the sterile atmosphere of the chip manufacturing plant, has a brother who is labouring in the fields. She uses the highest technology known to humanity; he uses the methods and tools that have endured for thousands of years. But the societies are in a constant social turmoil. As Table 4 shows, modern cities are sucking peasant labour in from the countryside and proletarianising it at an astonishing rate.[9] The social and political structures of such societies are necessarily under immense pressures. The beliefs and habits of past times do not disappear overnight, but at the same time new conditions of life produce the germs of new ideas and new horizons, as Marx and Engels famously observed in the *Communist Manifesto*.[10] This process of social transformation has been the immediate life experience of millions of people throughout South and East Asia. Born into a world of agriculture, they live in a world of industry. Born in villages, they live in cities. Born to obey the old ways, they struggle in a confrontation with the new.

TABLE 4: COMBINED AND UNEVEN DEVELOPMENT

Country	Agricultural workers as percentage of total labour force		Industrial workers as percentage of total labour force	
	1980	1990	1980	1990
China	76	74	14	15
Indonesia	59	57	12	14
Philippines	52	45	15	15
Thailand	71	64	10	14
Malaysia	41	27	19	23
(South) Korea	37	18	27	35
Hong Kong	1	1	50	37
Singapore	2	0	44	36
Japan	11	7	35	34

[Source: World Bank]

These structural changes have meant changes in the conditions of life of the masses. Workers in Japan, and increasingly in South Korea, have life experiences which in many respects are the same as those of workers in other advanced countries but, in those countries that have experienced growth more recently, the change to the new world is measurable in the vital statistics. Infant mortality in the region has fallen from 44 per 1,000 live births in 1987 to 35 in 1993. Life expectancy rose during the same period from 67 to 68 years, four years more than the developing countries' average of 64. Adult illiteracy fell from 29 percent in 1985 to 24 percent in 1990.[11] To take poverty alone, one study, using the criterion of an income of US$1 per day or less as a measure of absolute poverty, found that:

> The number of poor people in the region fell by 27 percent during 1975-1985, and 34 percent in 1985-1995—the fastest pace of poverty reduction in all of the developing world. In 1975, six out of ten East Asians lived in poverty; two out of ten do now. The region's most populous countries, China and Indonesia, alone held 92 percent of the region's poor in 1975. China's poverty incidence dropped by 63 percent, while Indonesia's poverty incidence fell by 82 percent. Other countries had similarly impressive achievements—Thailand's poverty incidence fell by 90 percent (from 8.1 to less than 1 percent), and Malaysia's fall was of 95 percent (from 17.4 to less than 1 percent).[12]

To be sure, this still leaves around 400 million people living in absolute poverty in the region, mostly in China, and it is entirely reasonable to say that the definition of 'poverty' is so desperately mean that the figures serve to conceal almost as much as they reveal. Despite the real gains, in the period 1989-1995, 17 percent of under-fives in China were malnourished. In Indonesia the figure was 39 percent, in the Philippines 30 percent, in Thailand 13 percent and in Malaysia 23 percent. Even in wealthy Japan the figure was 3 percent. For the working class and the peasants, the experience of capitalist industrialisation is a profoundly contradictory one. Some sections experience marginal but very real gains, while others see their already miserable conditions grow even more desperate. Uneven development means unevenness within the working class as much as anywhere else.

The other side of the coin, however, is the growth of a newly rich, indeed sometimes obscenely rich, capitalist class. Siti Hardianti Rukmana, President Suharto's eldest daughter, popularly known as Tutut, helped the national economy by handing over some of her gold and jewels: two kilograms of gold, to be precise. This was only a tiny fraction of her share of the family wealth that is estimated at US$40 billion.[13] To take another example, in Thailand:

> Consumerism was king. New Mercedes-Benz sales ranked third in the world. In 1995, the ratio of Benzes to all new cars sold in Thailand was 1:9, second only to Germany. New luxury boutiques opened throughout Bangkok, touting

the latest fashion lines and products from Paris, London and New York. If
products were not available locally, consumers shopped abroad. In the early
1990s, Thais became known as the global shoppers par excellence. Signs in
Thai could be seen adorning shop windows in Switzerland, France and Hong
Kong.[14]

It is certainly not the case that the only beneficiaries of this explosive
growth have been bankers and capitalists in New York, Tokyo or
London, nor are all of the local rich living off the rent of a natural
resource like oil, as is the Sultan of Brunei. Many of the people who
have profited from the labour of the new proletariat have been from the
very same villages as the people they employ. They are not outsiders bat-
tening on the local economy. They are not the 'tools of the world
bourgeoisie'. They are capitalists in their own right. They are independent exploiters who extract surplus value from the labour of their own
workforce. They have class interests of their own and they seek to
defend them. To be sure, they are not, for the most part, as powerful as
capitalists in New York or Tokyo, but neither are they their puppets. One
of the issues that has been at stake in this crisis has been a struggle to
work out exactly what the relationship is between these local, new born
capitalists and the bankers and politicians of the developed world.

Why did the economic miracle take place?

The sorts of changes to the social structure that we have looked at above
are the ones that normally accompany the transition to a modern capitalist economy, but they also illustrate one of the key elements that
helped to produce the rapid rates of growth. The widespread poverty prevailing even today in the countryside means that there is always a ready
supply of extremely cheap labour available for capitalist exploitation.
However desperate conditions may be in the new factories, and however
miserable the wages, the whip of rural poverty drives young men and
women off the land, into the cities and onto the labour market. It is estimated that there are 150 million people in the countryside who are under
employed. So compelling is this pressure that the Chinese government
has made it illegal to enter cities without official permission. Despite
that, around 70 million technically illegal workers crowd the urban
streets looking for employment.[15] Once in the cities, life may be harsh
and demanding, but it is certainly no worse, and, in booms at least, it is
marginally better than what went before.

This is no mysterious process that we need some special 'Asian'
factor to explain. It is exactly the same mechanism as that by which the
proletariats of Britain, the US and other advanced economies came into
being. The basements of Victorian Manchester, or the tenements of

Gilded Age New York, were grim indeed, but peasants from Ireland and elsewhere flocked into them, driven by the certainty of hunger and misery if they stayed where they were. The exploitation of a rural 'reserve army of labour' is a common feature of the earliest phase of the development of industrial capitalism in all countries. This widespread availability of cheap labour is one important factor explaining the growth of these economies. It means that in those labour intensive industries in which wage costs are the most important constituent of price, these economies can gain an advantage over higher wage countries. But low wages are not enough on their own to explain this growth. After all, labour is equally cheap in Bangladesh, or much of Africa, where there has been no such rapid transformation. Alongside the poverty of the working class, there have been a number of other factors that do indeed form a common pattern throughout the region.

The first of these is that in all of the countries there has been considerable repression, particularly directed against the left and the working class. In Japan there was a major working class offensive in the years after 1945, that was only defeated by an alliance between the US occupiers and their erstwhile Japanese enemies. The resulting anti-Communist crusade drove thousands of militant workers out of the factories, smashed many independent unions, and created the conditions for the tight control of labour that still exists in Japan. Other countries have had much more savage repression.

Thailand holds what must be the modern world record for the frequency of military violence, with 17 coups and attempted coups since 1945, but bloody military interventions have been central to the recent history of both Korea and Indonesia as well. Military rule in Korea, and the savage suppression of working class opposition there, is well known. Indonesia was, if anything, worse, albeit less well known. Bourgeois commentators usually refer coyly to Suharto having come to power 'in a period of civil unrest'. This little phrase covers an enormous massacre in 1965, of which the main victim was the Indonesian Communist Party, then the largest non-ruling Communist Party in the world. The Indonesia military leadership, in response to an attempted coup by leftist junior officers that had support from some members of the Communist Party, launched what one commentator described as:

> ...one of the biggest massacres since the Second World War. The top leadership of the party were all executed; the only member of the Politburo to survive was in Peking for health reasons. But the army also set out to destroy the base of the CP in the villages; the total figure for those killed was certainly well over a hundred thousand, and may have been as high as half a million. The technique adopted by the army was to go into a village and compel the headmen to give the names of all CP members and sympathisers,

round them up, and then inform the violently anti-Communist Christian and
Muslim mobs when they were to be released. As they came out of jail they
were cut to pieces with knives and choppers.[16]

The current rulers of Malaysia, too, have their origins in a war against
the Communists. In this case, it was a war waged by the British while
they were still the colonial rulers of the country. The imperialist victory
ensured that the people who came to power when the British withdrew
were reliable friends of private capitalism. The 'Republic of China' in
Taiwan, set up when the Kuomintang (KMT) was driven from the mainland in 1949, and established with a massacre of local oppositionists,
experienced one party rule and martial law up to the 1980s. The extent to
which the sworn enemies of the KMT, the Chinese 'Communist Party',
rules the mainland through the repression of any forms of opposition,
and particularly working class opposition, is notorious. Formal ideolo-
gies aside, one thing the rulers of the region have in common is ruthless
hostility to working class organisation and struggle. But that, as we know
only too well, is not at all an especially 'Asian' characteristic.

In all of these cases, the new working class that has been built up in
the years of expansion confronted a state machine that was only too
willing to use severe measures against anyone who openly dissented. It
was extremely difficult to build strong, independent unions, and where
they did emerge, as in South Korea, it was necessary to use the most
extreme forms of mass action to achieve any gains against an authori-
tarian management backed to the hilt by the state machine. As a result of
these circumstances, the ruling class throughout the region has often
been able to impose conditions that elsewhere in the world would have
met stern opposition. It is not that workers in the toy factories in the
Special Economic Zones in China do not mind being locked in at the
start of the shift and only let out at the end. They mind just as much as
workers anywhere else, particularly since they know very well from
recent incidents the horrendous consequences that these measures can
result in if there is a fire or other emergency. What they have lacked so
far is the organisation and power to do anything about it.

The second important factor is shared by many, but not all, of the
countries in question. The accidents of geography meant that during the
Cold War the region was one in which there was very heavy US involvement, always political and very often military. The first case was Korea,
where the modern state of South Korea owes its entire existence to the US
military, and which continues to this day to be home to 37,000 US soldiers, armed to the teeth with everything from handguns up to nuclear
weapons. The Korean War, which devastated the peninsula, also provided
a huge boost to the economy of Japan, then the most important staging
post for US forces. Later the direct and indirect economic benefits from

the US presence helped to provide a motor for growth in Korea itself. Taiwan, similarly, was for years entirely dependent for its existence on US military support, and was the recipient of substantial aid as well. After the US mended its fences with Beijing in the 1970s, it withdrew from its overt backing of Taiwan, but even as late as 1996, when the mainlanders staged threatening military manoeuvres, US warships were sent to the Straits of Taiwan as a warning not to go too far. All of the countries in the region, and in particular Thailand, which was a major rest and recreation centre, benefited economically from the protracted US involvement in Vietnam in the 1960s and 1970s.

The third, and today most problematic, factor that the countries of the region have in common is a close relationship between the state, banks and industry. This is not a uniquely South and East Asian phenomenon. Throughout the 20th century there has been a close union between these three elements in many different societies. The extreme form was the fusion of all three into a single bureaucratic state capitalist class that was characteristic of the Stalinist states, but weaker versions were, and are also to be found in countries with rabidly anti-Communist politics, such as the old white South Africa. The underlying rationale for this union was that local capitalists wished for, and perhaps needed, the protection and support of 'their' state machine in order to defend themselves against competitors. The state could control many things apart from repression, although that was indeed one of its main functions. It could control the flow of credit, and use formal and informal measures to direct investment into priority areas. In the case of Malaysia, for example:

> *Corporate reporting standards and the rights of minority shareholders, for example, fall well below those of most Western nations. It is partly for this reason that many of the more important Malaysian conglomerates were able to take out large bank loans to finance risky projects which now threaten to turn sour. Other issues of concern include the extent to which politically well-connected companies have been able to obtain major contracts in circumstances that are frequently less than transparent. National economic institutions such as the Central Bank, while more sophisticated than in many other countries in the region, are also quite open to manipulation for short term political purposes. Unfortunately, in times of political stability and strong economic growth, such matters are easily forgotten in the rush to make money.*[17]

The state could protect imports through tariffs, and provide incentives to exporters. It could, through its educational policies, provide the kinds of skilled labour that are needed to run modern industries. It could provide some of the elements of infrastructure, for example a modern telecommunications system, that are essential for any business that seeks to operate on more than the local scale. It could, in general, provide the conditions that local capital needed to get off the ground.

None of these functions, nor the corrupt ways that they were carried out, are unique to South and East Asia. Despite the claims of globalisation theorists, still, today, capital is everywhere closely intertwined with the state system and dependent upon it, but the shape and extent of the link in this region is now unusual. For one thing, it depends to a large extent on relationships mediated through the family and friendship networks, which is how it got its popular name of 'crony capitalism'. Indonesia is usually taken as the most notorious example of a more general trend, with Suharto's friends and relations enjoying local monopolies, owning banks, benefiting from state funding and so on.[18] For example, of the 16 banks that failed in 1997, three were owned by Suharto's immediate relatives.[19] Such links, however, were present in most of the countries in the region.

The rational core of all this, extending far beyond Indonesia, is that control over the banking system and industry allows firms to enter international markets from which they would otherwise be excluded by the pressure of competition, defend themselves against technically more advanced rivals located in more developed economies, and survive the long periods of low profits that are the inevitable result of trying to enter an established market.

In the case of the South and East Asian economies, there was an additional factor that is very important in explaining the rapid pace of growth. These are, as we have seen, societies experiencing rapid social change, in which uncertainty is a central existential component of people's lives. At the same time, they are societies without any developed form of social security. There is little or no state provision for unemployment and little or no provision for state pensions. In such circumstances, the only possible response for workers is to try to make provision for themselves. Although rapid growth meant that until recently the prospect of unemployment was relatively remote, sickness and old age are the inescapable lot of even the most devoted workers. The only way that an individual or family can make provision against them is through savings, and it is indeed the case that these societies have very high rates of savings. Again there is nothing particularly 'Asian' about saving—it is simply part of an attempt to make sure that one can continue to live even when it is not possible to work. In societies with a longer history of capitalist social relations, like Britain and the US, these 'savings' still take place, but it is through the relatively formal, socialised mechanisms of pension funds, health schemes, and the other forms of payment that sustain the welfare provisions that constitute the social wage.

High savings on their own, however, do not ensure high domestic investment. While it is axiomatically true that total saving equals total investment, there is no certainty that this will be concentrated within one country. What the saver, either individual or corporate, seeks is the best possible return on investment. Logically, if this can be obtained in another country, then that is where capital will flow. In other words, all things being equal, there should tend to be a uniform general level of return on investment around the world. One of the main functions of a closed banking system is that it interrupts this levelling process. Keeping out foreign bankers means that domestic savers have no option but to place their funds with the local banks. These, therefore, can set the returns for individual savers lower than the world market would dictate. They can thus ratchet up the total amount of savings needed to support a person in old age or sickness, and thus stimulate saving, while at the same time making generous loans to local industrialists at advantageous rates. In periods of expansion, they can turn this trick while still making a profit. One of the main reasons for the success of capitalists in the Tiger economies was that they gained a competitive advantage relative to the more open economies like the US precisely from their privileged access to large quantities of cheap capital.

Taken together, these factors meant that there was indeed an 'Asian model' of economic development, first pioneered by Japan and then followed to a greater or lesser extent by the other economies of the region. It began with an alliance of the state and local capital directing resources into labour intensive industries with a low technical threshold, aiming to enter the world market by undercutting established producers, and protecting infant industries through direct and indirect trade barriers. To finance this, at least in the initial stages, domestic savings generated out of acute social uncertainty were mobilised as cheap credit by a closed banking system that was closely linked to industrial capital. To the extent that they succeed in this, a new world division of labour emerges. Chemicals are a good example of this. One commentator wrote recently:

An East-West divide is opening up in the chemicals industry as low-cost manufacturers in South East Asia prepare to take a dominant share of the global commodity chemical market. Many European producers have decided that they cannot compete on production costs, and have spun off or sold their industrial businesses. They are concentrating instead on speciality chemicals. The changing shape of the industry reflects the different focuses of Eastern and Western manufacturing. Operations to produce commodity chemicals such as titanium dioxide and polyethylene tend to be relatively straightforward to set up and run. Consequently, the businesses are low-margin and prices are uniform. On the other hand, the manufacture of speciality products requires technical expertise. This makes it more difficult for new entrants to the sector to undercut established companies on production costs.[20]

This, however, is not the end of the story. What the capitalists of Japan could do in the 1950s, the capitalists of South Korea could do in the 1970s, and the capitalists of Thailand could do in the 1980s. There is a constant danger that someone else, with access to even cheaper sources of labour and even greater state protection, will undercut your market. Back in 1996, while everyone was still convinced that the Asian model was a good one, the World Bank drew attention to this problem: 'Rising wage costs, and emerging competition from even lower labour-cost countries means that East Asian countries will need to move up to more sophisticated markets to compete'.[21] Once the bulk of the very cheap labour has been sucked off the land, and it becomes necessary to reproduce an urban labour force, it also becomes necessary to raise wages, irrespective of the existence of an organised working class. If the generation that grew up in a pre-industrial economy could be worked to death at low cost because it cost the new capitalists nothing to produce, the next generation has to come from somewhere and, apart from relying on immigration, that implies paying a sufficiently high wage to allow successful human reproduction. As labour becomes more expensive, it becomes more and more important to economise in its use. Thus there is a tendency for those capitalists who have succeeded in entering the low value added markets to try to move up to more capital intensive, skill demanding, and profitable, kinds of production. This desire to move away from manufacturing T-shirts and trainers and to produce cars and aircraft is one of the reasons why the states of the region place such a heavy emphasis on education. It is the only way that they can get access to the kinds of skilled labour that are essential if such a move to more technologically sophisticated forms of production are to be accomplished.

TABLE 5: SOUTH KOREA'S EXPORTS AND IMPORTS

	1962	1985	1995
GNP (US$)	2.3 billion	90 billion	452 billion
Total exports (US$)	0.05 billion	30 billion	125 billion
Percentage primary goods	72.3	9.7	4.9
Percentage light industrial goods	27.7	36.9	22.5
Percentage heavy industrial goods	—	54.4	72.6
Total imports (US$)	0.42 billion	31 billion	135 billion
Percentage consumer goods	23.6	8.5	10.2
Percentage raw materials	54.0	55.9	50.0
Percentage capital goods	22.4	35.6	39.8

[*Source: South Korean government*]

Table 5 illustrates this process in general terms for the case of South Korea.[22] Although the absolute figures give an exaggerated picture, since they are not adjusted for inflation or exchange rate fluctuations, they do provide some sense of the scale of the growth. The figures for the percentages of imports and exports in different categories are, however, very clear. They show that the economy moved from being a very small exporter of primary goods (essentially raw materials) first, to the export of light manufactures, and finally the products of heavy industry. Thus by 1995 exports to the US, by far the largest single recipient of South Korean goods, were 56 percent made up of electronic goods.[23] In a competitive capitalist world economy, there are no stable and assured market niches. The factors which produced comparative advantage in one period can evaporate or move to another location in the next. Up to 1997 there was a sort of economic escalator in which first Japan, then South Korea and then the other countries of the region began with the most primitive forms of capitalist industrial production and then moved on progressively to more advanced, and more profitable, fields.

The basic economic model present here does therefore display some common 'Asian' features, but it is in itself a variant of a more general characteristic of the 20th century world economy. Capital develops on a national basis, but has to operate increasingly on a world market. In order to compete effectively in that market, it needs the aid of 'its own' state. Not only must that state keep the working class in its place, and provide the general conditions for successful capitalist production, but it is also a valuable source of protection against capitalists based in other states. There is no contemporary capitalist society in which this is not the case, not even the US. In other countries the phenomenon is present to a much greater degree. In the case of the Tiger economies and their emulators, the local state provided the protected conditions in which infant industries could thrive, ensured cheap and docile labour and cheap capital. These factors, combined with boom conditions in the world economy, have allowed a number of societies to build export oriented industrial economies of varying degrees of maturity. This may not be a 'normal' development, but it is hardly a mysterious one that requires recourse to semi-mystical concepts about those societies.

Why did the crisis occur?

If the model was such a successful one, sustaining the protracted colossal growth of the Japanese economy as well as the more modest achievements of other capitalist classes, why should it suddenly produce a major crisis? Bourgeois theorists give various answers to this, most of which are variants on the following astonishingly crude explanation:

At the root of the crisis in...East Asia in 1997 was a sudden change of heart on the part of investors in the world economy's industrial core—in New York, Frankfurt, London and Tokyo... In East Asia in 1996, international investors poured perhaps $100 billion into the region's economies. In 1998—even though East Asian currencies have been lowered far enough to create some equally amazing bargains for those seeking long-term investments—we will be lucky if the net private capital flow is zero... The root cause of the crises is a sudden change in international investors' opinions. Like a herd of not-very-smart cattle, they were all going one way in 1993 or 1996, and then they turned around. Was the stampede of capital in emerging markets disconnected from fundamentals of profit and business, or is the stampede of capital out an irrational panic? The correct answer is probably 'yes'—the market was manic, it is now panicked, and sudden change in opinion reflects a psychological victory of fear over greed.[24]

Pleasant though it would be to believe that our rulers are 'not-very-smart cattle' prone to easy panic, this sort of explanation really will not do. For one thing, it does not explain anything. Why should there be a change of heart? After all, even very dumb cattle only stampede when *something* scares them.

The Marxist account of the crisis sees the financial crisis as a symptom of underlying problems with the general economic situation. The most fundamental of these is the overall failure of the world system to find a method of orderly restructuring. This crisis is not unprecedented. There was a financial crisis in Europe, including Britain, during 1992-1993, then a crisis in Latin America in 1994-1995, and now a third in Asia, which will last we don't know how long. What, essentially, is at stake in all of these is a vast overcapacity on a world scale in a number of industries—allegedly 40 percent in automobiles, for example. The way that capitalism would 'naturally' resolve such a situation is for the weaker capitalists to go under. Firms would go bust. Banks would fail. Savings would be destroyed, and so on. There would be a great destruction of capital and, at the cost of vast human suffering for the working class, the system would be ready for another period of rapid expansion. This has not happened this time around. The major capitalist economies are very reluctant to allow big units of capital located in their own territorial patch to go bust. They prop up banks, bail out ailing companies, and try to make sure that some other state suffers the agonies of massive failure.

TABLE 6: REAL PERCENTAGE GROWTH RATES FOR JAPAN

Year	1990	1991	1992	1993	1994	1995	1996
Real GDP% growth	5.1	3.8	1.0	0.3	0.6	1.4	3.5

[Source: IMF]

The prime example of this at the moment is Japan. Since the collapse of the 'bubble economy' at the end of the 1980s, it has proved very difficult to get the economy to grow. As Table 6 shows, despite frequent reflationary packages, real GDP growth has been very low.[25] The fundamental reason for this is that it has proved politically impossible to force through the restructuring of the large number of banks that have loans that are no longer making payments ('non-performing loans'). The banks and the finance ministry have in fact proved very reluctant to reveal the true scale of these loans. In September 1997 they said they were around 22 trillion yen. Under pressure, in January 1998 they said they were around 76 trillion yen: 3.5 times higher. What the real figure is remains obscure. As one Japanese commentator put it:

> Information about bad loans is still vague and invites confusion rather than assurance. Stock and foreign exchange markets have been plagued by doubts about the health of certain banks and corporations. Rumours that some companies face a crisis have been enough to trigger panic selling of their stock and prompted depositors to withdraw funds. Firms targeted in this way have had difficulty securing credit, putting them at risk of collapse.[26]

The actual collapse, under the weight of its 3 trillion yen debt, of Yamaichi Securities, the fourth largest brokerage in Japan, on 24 November 1997, demonstrates just how deep the problems are facing Japanese companies. There is a steady drain of smaller banks and other companies closing. Figures for bankruptcies were at their highest since the Second World War in 1997.[27] What has not yet happened, however, is the kind of massive shake out that would be necessary to liquidate all of the bad debts. The Japanese government is slowly being forced by international capital into addressing the problems, but these problems worry even the IMF:

> The recent plan to inject public funds to bolster the Deposit Insurance Corporation represent an important step toward resolving the lingering problems of the Japanese banking sector. The goal of these measures is to ensure the stability of the banking system while advancing the needed resolution of the bad loan problem. Toward this end, it will be essential to ensure that the public funds are used to promote the needed bank restructuring rather than to support unviable institutions. A transparent and credible plan for using the funds to close insolvent institutions and to restructure undercapitalised banks, along with the government's plans for strengthening regulatory and disclosure standards, will lay the foundation for a successful transformation of Japan's financial system, as the 'big bang' initiative unfolds.[28]

The worry of the ruling classes outside Japan is that the political influence of their Japanese competitors will be used to bail them out long after the logic of capitalism would dictate bankruptcy. A life support system of state backed credit means that the beneficiaries can hold out longer than would otherwise be the case. They might even outlast capitalists elsewhere who do not have such support. The 'wrong' firms would then go bust. They would be 'wrong' in the sense that they might not be the economically less efficient, but just the poorly connected producers in a particular market. They would also be 'wrong' from the point of view of the capitalists elsewhere who owned them, and would lose out 'unfairly' in the competitive struggle.

TABLE 7: DESTINATIONS OF EXPORTS FROM SOME SOUTH EAST ASIAN COUNTRIES

Country of origin	Destination (percentage of total exports)		
	US	Japan	Europe
South Korea (1996)	17.6	12.2	16.5
(ROC) Taiwan (1994)	26.2	11	13.9
Hong Kong (1994)	25.4	5.3	17.4 (EU)
(Re-exports) (1996)	20.4	6.8	14.4 (EU)

[Sources: Governments of South Korea, Taiwan and Hong Kong]

The continuing slow growth in Japan had two important effects. In the first place, it meant that the Japanese yen fell somewhat against other currencies, particularly the US dollar. In 1994 the average exchange rate was around 100 yen to US$1; by 1997 the rate was around 120 yen per dollar. A 20 percent devaluation of the yen means that Japanese exports are cheaper on the world market, and particularly in the US, than they had been previously. This had a major effect in the rest of South and East Asia because many of the smaller economies had fixed their exchange rates relative to the US dollar, in an effort to attract foreign investment and deter currency speculation. Their export prices thus remained relatively stable. This was a particular problem because, as Table 7 shows, the destination of many of the manufactured goods from the Tigers and their emulators is the US and, to a lesser extent, Europe.[29] This meant that, while their substantial imports from Japan became cheaper, their relatively limited exports to Japan became absolutely more expensive. More importantly, the much greater proportion of their exports directed to third markets became relatively more expensive compared with those directed to the same markets, particularly from Japan. At the top end of the market, in the most advanced industrial sectors, these price shifts gave Japanese exporters a comparative advantage against their competitors in South and East Asia. Selling the same products into the same market, relative pricing is a vital component of competitive advantage. South Korea, for example, is particularly sensitive to moves of the yen against the dollar:

> The two largest Asian economies share many of the same exports, including electronics, steel, semiconductors, chemicals and automobiles. Over 50 percent of Korea's exports compete directly with Japanese products... Hence, the won's moves against the dollar often mirror the yen's trading movements versus the US currency, as local exporters vie to make their products more attractively priced compared with the products of their Japanese rivals.[30]

The prospects for continuing with an export oriented economy that could avoid the problem of even lower wage competitors undercutting it from below by continually moving up the scale of capital, technology and skill were thus made that much more difficult.

At the same time, a really formidable low wage competitor at the bottom end of the market was starting to make itself felt. China has not only grown very rapidly over the past decade, but has become very much more oriented on the world market: 'China is the tenth largest trading nation in the world and attracts more foreign direct investment than any country except the United States'.[31] The 1994 devaluation of the yuan (now the renminbi—the 'people's money') gave Chinese exporters a powerful advantage in those, essentially low technology, products in which it competes directly with other South and East Asian economies. By 1996 'Thailand began losing ground to China, particularly in labour-intensive sectors such as garments, footwear and parts'.[32] Overall a group of countries whose economies depended heavily on exports found themselves caught between increasing Japanese competition in the more sophisticated goods and increasing Chinese competition in the less sophisticated goods. The room for manoeuvre, at least with a fixed exchange rate, was greatly reduced. In country after country, but notably Thailand and South Korea, there was a mounting current account deficit as exports failed to cover imports for the first time in years.

The second major consequence of the slow growth of the Japanese economy is that there have been increasing capital outflows. Even while growing slowly, the Japanese economy is massive and generates vast surpluses, which need to find some kind of profitable home. The difficulty of finding reliably profitable investments in Japan has meant that finance capital has increasingly looked elsewhere for outlets. There has, in the 1990s, been a massive outflow of funds from Japan, mostly to other developed countries but also particularly to South and East Asian countries. Developing countries in Asia attracted US$108 billion in 1995 and nearly US$100 billion in 1996, and much of this came from Japan.[33] More and more capital, generated all around the world, found itself tempted to South and East Asia by what appeared to be assured profits arising from expanding economies and stable exchange rates. Much of this was foreign direct investment (FDI), going into new factories to churn out yet more goods for the world market. One new trend, however, was the development of foreign portfolio investment (FPI)—money just looking for a profitable home. Overall:

> *FDI grew from $1.3 billion (10 percent of net capital flows to East Asian countries) in 1980 to $43.0 billion, or 50 percent in 1994... FPI increased from nil to $18.1 billion, or 24 percent of capital flows, in the same period. East Asia is now the destination of over half of total direct and portfolio investment flows to all developing countries and is expected to remain the leading recipient region. In East Asian countries these flows now represent 3 percent of gross domestic product (GDP), or 10 percent of investment. Foreign capital from all sources accounts for about 15 percent of investment. This surge in private capital flows since the late 1980s has been the result of both 'pull' and 'push' factors—the former consisting of rapid growth and high rates of return in recipient countries and the latter of declining rates of return, fewer restrictions on foreign investment, and large pools investable in source countries. Recent regulatory changes in source countries have allowed the issuing of developing country securities in industrial country markets. Technological advances in communications and financial instruments make it much easier to undertake these transactions.[34]*

Some of these huge investment flows no doubt went into expanding production, but a substantial proportion went into stock market speculation, property price inflation, and what turned out to be dodgy loans to local companies. Massive investment in an economic system that is already under strain is a recipe for producing unsold goods—this is the root of the classic crisis of overproduction. We can see evidence of this building up when we look at the rates of growth for these countries, as shown in Table 8.[35]

TABLE 8: GROWTH IN REAL GDP FOR SELECTED COUNTRIES

Country	1991	1992	1993	1994	1995	1996	1997e
South Korea	8.46	4.70	5.80	8.60	9.00	7.10	5.95
(ROC) Taiwan	7.55	6.76	6.32	6.54	6.03	5.70	6.20
(PR) China	8.00	13.20	13.50	12.60	10.20	9.70 e	—
Malaysia	8.65	7.80	8.30	8.70	9.50	8.20	—
Thailand	7.89	7.40	7.80	8.80	8.60	6.70	2.00
Indonesia	6.62	6.10	7.25	7.48	8.20	7.80	6.00
Philippines	-1.00	-0.04	2.10	4.40	4.80	5.48 e	4.90
Singapore	—	6.04	10.10	10.10	8.90	7.00	6.50
Hong Kong	5.10	6.30	6.13	5.29	4.68	4.70	5.50

[Source: Political and Economic Risk Consultancy, e = estimate]

While all these figures are very high compared with those for Japan shown in Table 6, or for those of any other highly developed country for that matter, they mostly show a peak of expansion in 1994 and 1995, followed by a slowdown in 1996. In other words, while the economies had not actually contracted, the speed of expansion had been noticeably reduced. This was the result of a sharp decline in new investment, as perceptions of the possibilities for future profits evaporated. As one Korean economist noted, just before the storm broke:

Facility investments [ie investments in plant and machinery—CS] *of Korean companies increased by 15.7 percent in 1996, compared to 36.7 percent and 37.9 percent growth recorded in 1994 and 1995 respectively. Behind this low increase was mainly completion of large projects which began or were in-process between 1994 and 1995 and production capacity increase already in place, together with discouraged investment plans due to a deterioration in the overall national economy.*[36]

Not only were investment plans put on hold, but an increasing proportion of production was stockpiled in lieu of being sold—up to 20 percent of the total in late 1996.[37] It was only in July 1997 that the rate of growth of these stockpiled goods fell below 10 percent (to 9.6 percent) for the first time since July 1995.[38] For two years South Korean companies were producing more and more, and not selling all of it. This, of course, leads to cash flow problems on a grand scale. So companies found themselves forced to borrow more and more money to keep themselves afloat, and they obtained much of this in short term loans from foreign banks, thus adding to the mounting foreign debt of the region.

In Thailand too there were the seeds of a crisis. Much of the portfolio investment that had poured in during the 1990s had found its way into property speculation, leading to a rash of speculative building projects.

By late 1996:

> *Reports began to surface that small developers were beginning to have difficulties in servicing their loans to local financial institutions. Poor sectoral research and over-enthusiatic credit officers helped fuel construction of unneeded property developments priced with unrealistic cash-flow projections... Developers came under increasing cash flow difficulties as local financial institutions cut back their financing lines while the number of unsold units rose... In February [1997], Somprasong Land became the first Thai company to default on a Euro-convertible debenture, a popular method for local firms to access cheap foreign funding.*[39]

In construction the mechanism of crisis is extremely clear. In the boom years it seemed as though property investments were a certain way to make a profit, and thus capital flooded into the sector. Vast numbers of offices, shops and houses were started. By late 1995 there were simply too many buildings being completed for them all to be profitably let or sold. As a consequence, the weakest and most exposed building companies started to fold: 'By 1995, an oversupply of housing emerged... With loans increasingly expensive and hard to get...the sector began to collapse in 1996'.[40]

Thus, when speculators first attacked the Thai bhat in February 1997, the grounds for a currency crisis were thoroughly prepared. All the economies were, by their standards, growing relatively slowly. There was substantial overcapacity on a world scale for several of the industries—steel, electronic goods, petrochemicals, semiconductors—that had been staples of the export drives. Exchange rate movements had eroded price advantages in key markets. Local companies found themselves unable to shift goods and borrowed more and more to stay afloat. The balance of payments situations were deteriorating. These are the conditions in which a speculative attack on a currency can be successful. Currency traders speculate on a daily basis against each and every tradable currency in the world. Usually their efforts are only of marginal effect—although quite large enough for them to make a great deal of money. These trades only become a crisis when there is a fundamental problem of an artificial exchange rate that no longer corresponds to the real economy. Far from being some kind of very stupid animal, Soros and his cohorts can see a weak economy even when the IMF cannot and, like the good capitalists that they are, they strive to turn a buck. The occasion of the crises in South and East Asia may have been a burst of currency speculation, but the causes lay in the fundamental weaknesses of the economies themselves.

What happens now?

The ruling class is divided. International bankers want their cash back. That is what the IMF is trying to make sure happens in each and every capital in the region. The local capitalist class, however, wants to survive with as much of its assets intact as possible. These two groups are struggling with each other over who is going to get what. The political crises of the region are vivid indicators of that battle.

The results of the currency crises have been massive devaluations, most spectacularly of the Indonesian ruppiah, but also of almost every other major currency in the region apart from the Hong Kong dollar. The effects have been devastating. Thailand was the first country to devalue, on 2 July 1997. Non-performing loans are estimated at 25 percent of the total.[41] Only two out of the 58 financial institutions that were closed have sufficient capital to reopen.[42] There have also been a string of cancelled projects—all 63 major projects were cancelled from July to December 1997, mostly in chemicals, paper, plastics and steel.[43] Cancelled projects and reduced orders mean redundancies. The Thai Employers Confederation estimates that in six categories of employment (garments, textiles, electronics, car parts, construction and services) 180,000 jobs went up to December. Perhaps 10 percent of all Thai jobs are at risk.[44]

The devaluations are intended to stimulate exports, but they also have the short term effect of making the economic situation for companies much worse. Many of the loans they obtained before the crisis in order to keep afloat were denominated in US dollars. The capital and interest have to be repaid in US dollars. The devaluation of local currencies makes that debt burden all the greater and accelerates the prospect of bankruptcy. On the other hand, devaluation might not provide so much of a boost to exports as has been hoped. Many of the goods exported depend on working up and re-exporting semi-finished products from more advanced countries, notably Japan. The devaluation of the currency means that those input prices increase, and thus the scope for price advantages in the finished article is much reduced.

Endangered local capitalists thus turn to their own state to ask for a bail out. Since there are very close connections between politicians and businessmen, as indeed there are elsewhere, these pleas for help have often been answered. The initial response of the South Korean government, for example, was to bail out the ailing car manufacturer Kia by, effectively, nationalising it. The extraordinary manoeuvres of Suharto, his odious family and his toadies, have been based on just that desire to keep their access to the honeypots. One commentator, writing between the onset of the crisis in 1997 and the much stricter terms imposed by the IMF in early 1998, noted that:

Several of the big ticket projects still slated to go ahead symbolise exactly what is wrong with the Indonesian economy. They include Tommy Suharto's national car project (made possible by massive tax concessions to a company with little experience in automobile manufacture and no local production facilities), Research and Development Minister Habbie's expensive N-250 aircraft development project and plans by Tutut, the president's daughter, to build a US$2.3 billion triple decker toll road and mass transit railway in Jakarta.[45]

The terms of the various support packages sponsored by the IMF have been in large measure designed to prevent this sort of thing, and to make sure that the economies in question put the interests of the international capitalist class before the pet projects of local politicians and businessmen.

These policies have led to some rifts among our rulers. The international capitalist class all want their money back, and a chance to make any windfall profits that might be going, but there are some differences of emphasis. South Korea is a case in point. The IMF, primarily an agency for US capital, has been stressing the need for stern financial discipline, but some of the biggest creditors, primarily European, have been taking a softer line. This is partly a question of how much it will hurt. European bankers are owed US$33.8 billion, Japanese bankers are owed US$24.3 billion, and US bankers are owed just US$9.36 billion. A hard line, raising interest rates and tightening the money supply, means that many South Korean companies will go bust, banks as much as industrial concerns. This will, of course, mean that there is no chance of Western and Japanese creditors getting the cash they are owed back in full. The bankers who have got most to lose are, naturally enough, the ones who are least enthusiastic about the application of the classical mechanisms of capitalism to their debtors. There is always the risk that such drastic measures will backfire on the lending countries, particularly Japan, and transform a regional problem into a full fledged world recession. The public criticisms of the harsh IMF regime, even when couched in technical terms, reflect this fundamental division of interest.

There is, however, much greater unanimity over other things. The first is that the local capitalist classes will have to reform themselves and allow much greater scope for their competitors. In country after country the IMF has made as a condition for its intervention a reform of the banking and finance system, particularly in order to allow foreign capital to purchase the devalued assets of the local economy. It has also been keen to dismantle protective measures, most obviously the scandalous ones like the monopolies that Suharto granted his family and friends over vital sectors of the economy, but also all of the other more normal barriers to trade. No one outside the IMF and the local finance ministries knows exactly what has been agreed, since the IMF does not publish the full text of its dealings with governments. What is clear from the public record, however, is that the terms for the bail out include very stringent conditions to ensure that the outcomes of the various rescue programmes are restructuring rather than repairing the existing set up. The key conditions for the January 1998 deal with Indonesia included a restructuring of the banking system, abolishing local monopolies in sugar and cloves, deregulating the trade in agricultural products, dissolving the cartels in cement, paper and plywood, and removing all barriers to foreign investment in palm oil.[46] When the first bail out plan for South Korea was agreed, Stanley Fischer, first deputy managing director of the IMF, gave a press conference. One of the exchanges ran as follows:

Question: IMF financial assistance goes to the treasury, into the reserves, but many of the big business conglomerates may experience financial difficulty stemming from ambitious expansion plans. How do we know that the money will not be used to shore up the finances of the conglomerates?
Fischer: This money is intended to bolster reserves and to assist in restoring confidence. For the rest, there is a well-defined fiscal programme that includes and defines whatever support—and it is practically nil—is to be given to the corporate sector.[47]

It is quite clear in South Korea and elsewhere that the aim of the IMF package is to 'restore confidence' in an economy at whatever human cost. Only that way, they argue, can normal capitalist relations be restored. The special interests of sections of the local ruling classes will have to be sacrificed to this greater good.

The thing that the capitalist class, national and international, is unanimous about is that the working class is going to have to pay for the crisis. Devaluation raises the price of imported goods, and thus reduces living standards. The 'rationalisation' of industry and the banks means the sacking of thousands, if not millions, of workers:

According to investment funds and business consultants in the region, Indonesia will shed two million jobs this year, Korea about 1.5 million, Thailand over one million, about 150,000 in Malaysia, close to 100,000 in the Philippines, and probably 20,000 in Singapore.[48]

All of this will take place in countries without even the modest welfare provisions that we take for granted in more developed countries, and where workers' personal savings are at risk from inflation and bank failure. Misery will follow in the wake of the IMF as surely in Asia as it has done in Latin America, Africa and Eastern Europe. As Lenin remarked, there is no crisis so deep that it cannot be resolved, provided that the working class can be made to pay for it. The big question is: will the ruling classes in South East Asia be able to solve their problems at the working class's expense?

The prospects for resistance

We have seen that it is a mistake to consider the countries of South and East Asia as one homogeneous entity, so we would expect to find that the chances of working class resistance differ from country to country. This is true, but, just as there are some general features of the way in which capitalism has developed in the region, there are also some general background features to the class struggle.

The most important of these is that the very pace of the transition in the later developers has made the hold of the ruling class over society relatively insecure. Among the 'ancient and venerable prejudices' that have been swept away by the hurricane of capitalist development were those that taught the poor that their lives would always be the same and that nothing could be done about it. The former peasant, uprooted from the farm, driven into the city, transformed into a wage worker, trained to use a modern machine, living in a gerry built tower block, knows from personal experience that things can be different, and that what people do makes a difference to society. Societies experiencing the rapid transition to industrial capitalism are always vulnerable to working class revolt precisely because the harsh routines of daily life, that workers in more established societies take reluctantly for granted, are seen as new, and perhaps temporary, impositions by the newly minted proletarians of a developing country.

Conditions of economic crisis make those stresses more acute. Not only are there the material hardships of unemployment and wage cuts to be endured, but the ruling class has lost one of its main ideological weapons. During the boom years, when people questioned the contrast between the vast wealth of the ruling class and the harsh conditions of the working class, the rulers could always reply that at least they were leading the country away from enslavement by the West and towards a more prosperous and developed future. Economic defeat, similar but much less intense than military defeat, always exposes the pretensions of rulers. What they have done no longer seems to be the only road to success, and the sacrifices they demand no longer seem so justifiable. The economic crisis exposes the claims of the ruling class to be following the only policies that are in the best interests of the whole of society. What to do next becomes an urgent question of public debate.

It does not follow that the answer the mass of the population will give to that great question is, overthrow capitalism and build a socialist society. The ruling classes have a few more very powerful ideological weapons in their arsenal that they can use to divert mass discontent from their own doors. Many of these are depressingly familiar to militant workers around the world. At the very start of the crisis, Mahathir Mohamad, prime minister of Malaysia, borrowed one of the most sordid pages from the book of tricks written by his former colonial masters when he argued that the currency crisis was the result of a 'Jewish plot'. This claim in South East Asia is even more ludicrous than it was in Europe 70 years ago, but other possible scapegoats are closer to hand. The vast movements of population that accompany industrial developments do not respect borders. There are hundreds of thousands of workers in the countries of South Asia who were born elsewhere and have travelled, legally or illegally, to Malaysia, Thailand and other centres of development, in the hope of finding work.[49] Just as the Nazis in Europe try to use the existence of migrant populations to split the working class, so the ruling classes in South Asia are saying that they will first drive out the migrants in order to ensure that 'their' workers retain their jobs.

Equally repellent, and equally dangerous, is anti-Chinese sentiment. This really is very close to the sort of racism that was used by the Nazis in Europe in the 1930s. In South Asia the Chinese diaspora has played a similar role to that which Abraham Leon argued the Jews had played in Central and Eastern Europe: they were a 'people-class' who were the cutting edge of the money economy. As a consequence, the Chinese form a substantial section of the capitalist class and of the professions. Again, like the Jews in Europe, they also form a substantial section of the proletariat and provide many of the leaders of the socialist movement. One of the standard techniques of the ruling class is to divert anti-capitalist sentiment into anti-Chinese sentiment. This has a long pedigree. The British won their colonial war in Malaysia mainly because they were able to portray the Communists as Chinese, and thus to isolate them from the mass of the Malay population. The 1965 massacre in Indonesia was, partly at least, an anti-Chinese pogrom. There is, sadly, evidence that this old poison still works. Some of the discontent in Indonesia this time around has found expression in anti-Chinese rioting. There were riots in Banayuwangi and Jember in Eastern Java on 16 January and in Kragan in Central Java some 800 young people, allegedly from a Muslim boarding school, attacked and damaged 20 shops on 26 January. All of these attacks had an anti-Chinese element.[50]

Elsewhere, in China itself for example, this exact strategy obviously cannot work, but there are other variants that have the same effect of dividing the working class. The history of China, Taiwan and Korea makes Japan, within living memory the occupying imperialist power, the target for nationalist sentiment. And in Japan itself memory of defeat at the hands of the US can still be utilised for these purposes. Throughout the region the harsh terms imposed by the IMF, and the fact that is so clearly the agent of the West, indeed of the US, give anti-imperialist rhetoric from the ruling class a real popular echo. It is, regrettably, everywhere the case that the ruling class can find the scapegoats they want.

This kind of rhetoric can be particularly dangerous when the left is, for whatever reason, not in a position to provide a coherent alternative. As we have seen, many of these countries have been very repressive, and almost everywhere the socialist movement is in a small minority. Nevertheless, there have been signs of resistance. In Japan itself, the largest and thus ultimately the most important of the economies, there has as yet been no sign that the isolated incidents of discontent are coalescing into a coherent oppositional movement. Elsewhere the picture is a little better. In Thailand, for example, 3,000 workers in an auto parts factory went on strike against a wage cut on 21 January. They blocked the roads around the plant and fought a long battle with the riot police. In China, despite severe repression, there is evidence of discontent. As the following poem, found in a magazine at a train station, shows, there are certainly plenty of people who are not at all happy with the recent economic 'successes'.

The Ten Successful Chinese

The first type is a dignitary. When trouble comes, there's sanctuary.

The second type is a public servant. Travels about in search of merriment.

The third type rents a business. Eating, drinking, whoring, gambling—all in the expenses.

The fourth type is a landlord. Cheating, duping, queering, frauding—and on the side a bawd.

The fifth type is a famous singer. Ticket sales and wealth beyond measure.

The sixth type is an entrepreneur. All earnings and losses his to endure.

The seventh type is a propagandist. Gluts his maw at all the banquets.

The eighth type is a famous painter. Draws crabs and shrimps and grows the richer.

The ninth type wears a police helmet. Eats from the plaintiff and the defendant.

The tenth type is the rest of the population. We study Lei Feng and make revolution.

[*From: 'Laugh—or Cry' in* **Far East Economic Review**, *15 January 1998, p49*]

The sentiments expressed clearly articulate a deep discontent with the people who have profited from capitalist development. More directly political dissidents face harsh persecution. On 16 January 1998 police in Datong, in the northern Shanxi province, arrested Li Qingxi for attempting to form an independent trade union. The 41 year old unemployed man, formerly a worker at the health clinic of the Datong Coal Mine administration, wrote and pasted up a 'Declaration of Foundation of Free Trade Unions'. A second activist, Zhao Changqing of the Nuclear Industry General's Number 813 factory in Hanzhong, was arrested a few days earlier. His crime was to take the constitution seriously and put himself forward as a candidate in the local elections. Factory officials told him that only Communist Party cadres above the rank of vice factory director could be nominated, and the police arrested him for protesting.[51] As the example of 'Solidarity' in Poland showed 20 years ago, courageous individuals like this have a well of support amongst ordinary workers that, in the right circumstances, can explode into mass action and organisation. Should the crisis spread to China, it could well provide the spark for such a conflagration.

In all of these cases, however, we are dealing with limited protests which, while they are evidence of discontent, do not yet amount to open, class conscious opposition. There is one country in the region, deeply affected by the crisis, where we know that there is much more substantial opposition. The South Korean working class has managed to establish legal organisations. It has a fine record of struggle, and there is every indication that there is mass opposition to the sackings and austerity that the ruling class is attempting to impose on the country as the price of recovery. In another article in this issue of *International Socialism*, Shin Gyoung-hee looks in detail at the response of the Korean working class, its organisations, their strengths and their weaknesses, and at the prospect of revolutionary socialist ideas finding a wider audience in the struggle. Here we need only note that South Korea is the key to the international situation. If the working class in that country can successfully resist the attacks upon its living standards, then not only will the South Korean ruling class and the IMF have suffered a defeat, but an example will have been given that can be copied all over South and East Asia, and far beyond. There can be no better answer to the ruling class lies about the 'Asian way' than a victory for the Korean working class.

Notes

1   According to reports, they had been extensively wined and dined, and taken to strip clubs, by representatives of companies wanting advance information on bank inspections: 'In full glare of live national television on Monday prosecutors raided Japan's most powerful ministry and arrested two banking regulators for receiving bribes and lavish entertainment at night spots in return for prior

intimation about surprise inspection of these banks' branches and other favours. On Tuesday, prosecutors launched another series of raids, this time on offices of the Dai-ichi Kangyo Bank, Asahi Bank, Sanwa Bank, and the failed Hakkaido Takushoku Bank', F Khergamvala 'Japanese Minister Quits' in *The Hindu*, 29 January 1998, p16. They were only the most recent in a series of very high profile cases, involving, for example, the finance director of the state Highway Agency, Takehiko Isaka, who had received massive amounts of 'entertainment' from Nomura Securities Co, in the expectation that it would be nominated as the lead broker in a bond issue. Many Japanese businessmen cannot see what is wrong with this. Nomura itself reported that it allocated 3.9 billion yen (around £20 million) for corporate entertainment in its recent accounts: 'Wining, Dining "Essential" Part of the Job?', *Daily Yomiuri*, 20 January 1998, p2.

2   The World Bank Group, *Annual Report 1997: East Asia and Pacific* (Washington DC, World Bank Group, 1997), pp1-2.

3   J Bartholet, 'The Won Is Not the Problem', *Newsweek*, 19 January 1998, p14. One should recall that this man is writing about a country that has been politically and military dependent on the US for much of the period since the Second World War. So long as the profits rolled in, this sort of thing was not even mentioned.

4   There are one or two dissenting voices, amongst them Martin Wolf, who wrote in the *Financial Times*: 'Conventional wisdom suggests the lesson is that East Asians should become as Western as possible as quickly as possible. This is the philosophy underlying the programmes of the International Monetary Fund. Yet the cardinal East Asian mistake could well be not that they liberalised too little, but rather that they liberalised too much and, above all, too imprudently'.'Caging the Bankers', 20 January 1998, p18.

5   S Cockerill and C Sparks, 'Japan in Crisis', *International Socialism* 72, Autumn 1996, pp27-58.

6   The data in this table are for 1995, and are taken from the World Bank *World Development Report* (Washington DC: World Bank, 1996), Tables 1 and 12, except for Taiwan, which is not allowed to be a member. These figures are for 1994, and are from ROC (1998), *The Republic of China at a Glance*, http://www.freesun.be/ ROC2.html.

7   Sources as in note 2, Tables 4 and 12, except for Germany, for which the source is OECD *Statistical Tables* (Paris: OECD, 1997).

8   Ibid, Table 11.

9   Ibid, Table 4.

10   K Marx and F Engels, *Collected Works*, vol 6 (London: Lawrence and Wishart, 1976), p487.

11   World Bank, *The World Bank Annual Report 1996* (Washington DC: World Bank, 1997), p82.

12   The World Bank Group, *Everyone's Miracle? Revisiting Poverty and Inequality in East Asia* (Washington DC: World Bank, 1997), News Release No 98/1448EAP. 1.

13   'Suharto Consulted Children On Reforms, Daughter Says', *Daily Yomiuri*, 20 January 1998, p7.

14   'Greed', *Bangkok Post Economic Review*, 1997, p2.

15   P Yatsko and M Forney, 'Demand Crunch', in *Far East Economic Review*, 15 January 1998, p46.

16   I Birchall, *Workers Against the Monolith* (Pluto Press, 1974), pp165-166.

17   Political and Economic Risk Consultancy (1997), *Country Risk Report: Malaysia*, http://www.asiarisk.com/mal.html.

18   The use of informal networks to coalesce a ruling class is not, of course, an Asian speciality. Britain has its 'old school tie' system with a similar function.

19   Political and Economic Risk Consultancy (1997), *Country Risk Report: Indonesia*, http://www.asiarisk.com/indo.html.

20   M Peel, 'East and West Go Separate Ways', *Financial Times Survey*: Global
     Business Outlook, 13 January 1998, vi.
21   G Kaji, *Sustaining the East Asian Miracle: The Prospects for Rapid Growth*,
     Plenary Session Speech to the World Economic Forum 1996 Europe/East Asia
     Summit, Hong Kong, 19 November 1996.
22   Government of South Korea, *Business in Korea: Economic Statistics* (1998),
     http://korea.emb.washington.dc.us/new/business/econ/Econostat1.htm.
23   Ibid.
24   J Bradford Delong, 'Corral the Biannual Crises', *Los Angeles Times*, 28 January
     1998. J Bradford Delong is not some dumb journalist but a full fledged professor
     of economics at the University of California, Berkeley. He is joined by some other
     famous names from the world of bourgeois economics. Jeffrey Sachs, the man
     who introduced 'shock therapy' to the former Communist world, for example,
     wrote, 'There is no "fundamental" reason for Asia's financial calamity except
     financial panic itself. Asia's need for significant financial sector reform is real, but
     not a sufficient cause for the panic. Asia is reeling not from a crisis of
     fundamentals, but from a self-fulfilling withdrawal of short-term loans.' 'IMF is a
     Power Unto Itself', *Financial Times*, 11 December 1997.
25   IMF, 'IMF Concludes Article IV Consultation with Japan'. Press Information
     Notice 97/19, 13 August 1997, http://www.imf.org/external/np/sec/pn/
     1997/PN9719.htm. 4.
26   J Hayakawa, 'Banks Must Open Up the Books or Suffer a Costly Trust Deficit',
     Daily Yomiuri, 21 January 1998, p7.
27   *Kyodo News*, 'Corporate Bankruptcy Debt Hits Postwar High in 1997', *Daily
     Yomiuri*, 20 January 1997, p12.
28   M Camdessus, 'Camdessus Welcomes Measures Announced by the Japanese
     Government', IMF News Brief No. 97/31.
29   The figures should be taken as indicative only, given the differences of date and
     definition that are indicated in the table. The sources are: Korean Embassy,
     Business in Korea: Economic Statistics (1998), http://korea.emb.washington.dc.
     us/new/business/econ/Econostat1.htm ; Government of Hong Kong, *Hong Kong in
     Figures: External Trade* (1998), http://www.info.gov.hk/censtatd/hkstat/hkinf/ex-
     trade.htm; Government of ROC, *The Republic of China at a Glance* (1998),
     http://www.freesun.be/ROC2.html.
30   Asia Chronology, *Chronology of the Asian Currency Crisis and its Global
     Contagion* (1998), http://www.stern.nyu.edu/~nroubini/asia/AsiaChronology1.
     html, 7.
31   The World Bank Group, *Country Brief: China* (Washington: The World Bank
     1997), p1.
32   'Exports', *Bangkok Post Economic Review* 1997, p3.
33   World Bank *Annual Report 1996* (Washington DC: World Bank Group, 1997),
     p82; S Fischer, *The Asian Crisis: A View from the IMF*. Address by Stanley
     Fischer at the Midwinter Conference of the Bankers' Association for Foreign
     Trade (Washington DC, 22 January 1998).
34   The International Bank for Reconstruction and Development, *Managing Capital
     Flows in East Asia Summary*. (Washington DC: World Bank Group, 1995), 5. To
     be fair, this was one of the few analyses to concentrate on the problems generated
     by this growth.
35   Political and Economic Risk Consultancy Ltd, *Country Risk Reports* (1998),
     http://www.asiarisk.com/.
36   G S Jeong, 'Forecast on 1997 Facility Investment', *Korean Development Bank
     Economic and Industrial Focus*, March 1997.
37   See Reuters' *Business Briefing: South Korea*, 1 April 1997, p2.

38   Kim, S and Kang, W, 'The Recent Trends and Forecast of Korean Economy',
      Korean Development Bank Economic and Industrial Focus, September 1997. 1.
39   'Greed', *Bangkok Post Economic Review*, op cit, p3.
40   'The Economy', *Bangkok Post Economic Review* 1997, p2.
41   'Banking and Finance', *Bangkok Post Economic Review*, op cit, p1.
42   'Greed' *Bangkok Post Economic Review*, op cit, p7.
43   'Investment', *Bangkok Post Economic Review*, op cit, p1.
44   Political and Economic Risk Consultancy, *Country Risk Report: Thailand* (1997),
      http://www.asiarisk.com/thail.html.
45   Political and Economic Risk Consultancy, *Country Risk Report: Indonesia (1997)*,
      p2. http://www.asiarisk.com/indo.html.
46   M Camdessus, Press Conference, 16 January 1998, p2.
47   IMF, 'Fischer Press Conference: Aim of Korean Program is to Staunch Immediate
      Crisis, Permit Return to Stability and Growth', *IMF Survey*, vol 26, no 23, 15
      December 1997, p387.
48   V Jayanth, 'A Breeding Ground for Dissent and Social Unrest', *The Hindu*, 28
      January 1998, p17.
49   'Dollars and Dolours', *Economist*, 24 January 1998, p30.
50   'Mobs Attack Shops in New Wave of Looting', *Hong Kong Standard*, 18 January
      1998.
51   'Activist Arrested for Poll and Trade Union Demands', *Hong Kong Standard*, 18
      January 1998, p5.

The crisis and workers' movement in South Korea

SHIN GYOUNG-HEE

Only ten months before the crash in South Korea mainstream economic commentators and analysts were still admiring South Korea's economy. Jeoffrey Sachs at Harvard University, adviser to the IMF and most famous preacher of free market economics, argued in South Korea's most influential bosses' paper, 'Since the economic structure of Korea is fundamentally different from that of Mexico, there is no possibility of recurrence of the situation that happened to Mexico'.[1] Paul Samuelson said, 'Most economic specialists [including himself] predict that this year's growth rates of East Asian economies will be higher again than are expected'.[2] As for the IMF, it could see 'no problem in Korea's economy in light of macroeconomic indexes such as international payments, growth rate, prices, and so on'.[3]

But right after the bankruptcy of Hanbo *chaebol* (conglomerate), some pro-capitalist media commentators suddenly began to see the problems. The *Financial Times* on 4 February 1997 indicated that 'Korean banks are in financial difficulties because of the insolvent obligation which is estimated to be some 8 percent of the total credit and because of fall in stock prices'.[4] And *Business Week* on 24 February 1997 also warned of the weakness of Asian banks. According to the *New York Times*, South Korean capitalists themselves began to have 'a sense of total crisis because of the slowing economic growth rate, declining stock market, decreasing currency value of the won, increasing trade deficit, and cumulative bad bonds of financial institutions'.[5]

Michel Camdessus, managing director of the IMF, nonetheless said in May 1997, 'The fundamentals of Korea's economy themselves are sound'.[6] Even on 14 August 1997, when the South East Asian economies ('Tiger cubs') were experiencing the crash and Kia, the eighth largest business group in South Korea, was faced with bankruptcy, the IMF estimated that next year the growth of the South Korean economy would increase to 9 percent. Not until late October when Hong Kong's stock market crashed and Kia finally proved to be bankrupt, only to be nationalised, did the international financial market eventually lose all confidence in South Korea's economic prospects.

Media pundits, as supporters of orthodox economics, try to explain this situation in *purely* financial terms as if financial markets have *nothing* to do with the 'objective economy'—the production and distribution of industrial wealth. But back in December 1995 the then new minister of finance and economy, Nah Woong-bae, acknowledged the 'seriousness of the economic situation' and later laid bare his heart saying, 'Problems are so intricate that I am at a loss what to do'.[7] The collapsing price for computer chips was the detonator. From early 1996 the global semiconductor market was in a state of 'oversupply' and the prices of South Korea's chips plummeted. Chips account for a quarter of South Korea's exports. South Korea's other principal exports—cars, ships, steel and petrochemicals—were all faced with a glut in the world market.[8] But more fundamental was the declining competitiveness of South Korean capital. Worsening international payments meant that South Korea's external liabilities at the end of 1997 proved to be over $200 billion.[9] More striking was the fact that 58.8 percent of the external liabilities were a short term loan payable within a year.

This combination of pressure from global overproduction by heavy and petrochemical industries and South Korea's own weakening competitiveness meant, for an export led economy, a profitability crisis. The net profit of listed firms in 1996 dropped by 55 percent compared with the previous year.[10] The falling profit rate must have been much starker in 1997, given the crash which happened in late October and continued into this year. The rate of ordinary profit to sales of manufacturing industry in 1996 was 1 percent as compared with 3.6 percent in 1995. The rate of increase in sales itself dropped from 20.4 percent to 10.3 percent. Already in 1995 ordinary profit and net income for the year of listed firms—except Samsung Electronics, Posco and Korea Electric Power Corporation—decreased respectively by 8.3 percent and by 3.8 percent, as compared with the previous year.[11] The rate of profit (as opposed to the mass of profit) becomes all the more important because South Korean firms have depended on borrowing. Chris Harman has elaborated this point:

Now the rate of profit regains its importance. For only if they get an adequate rate of profit can individual state capitals and individual multinational corporations pay the internationally determined rate of interest they owe to the banks. Nationally based accumulation cannot proceed unless it can match internationally determined standards of profitability.

Unless the national capital or the multinational corporation can meet these minimum standards it is operating at a loss once it has paid off its interest. And for a national economy to operate at a loss is to contract rather than expand. The emergence of international finance capital means that we have entered the age of the state capitalist recession.

As in the classical capitalist crisis, the tendency is for the internationally prevailing rate of interest to move in the opposite direction from the average international rate of profit. As profitability falls, the supply of funds to the banks gets tighter, yet more capitals get into difficulties which make them look to the banks for yet greater borrowing; the demand for funds rises faster than the supply, and interest rates soar, putting still further pressure on individual capitals.

The phase of capitalist history in which national capitals could ignore low profit rates by retreating into themselves is over. The old structure of the capital market—and the role played in this by financial capital—has re-emerged, at a higher, international level. Whole states are driven to abandon their half-finished investments at enormous cost, out of fear that they will not yield the level of profitability needed to pay off the bankers. The whole world becomes drawn into a single rhythm of half-hearted expansion of investment and convulsive contraction, of short, limited booms and long depressions.[12]

Until the late 1980s the average rate of net profit of South Korea's manufacturing industry was higher than that of Japan's, the US's and Europe's. But it has tended to fall during the three decades since industrialisation started in 1963. See the table and graph below:

AVERAGE RATE OF NET PROFIT OF MANUFACTURING INDUSTRY

	South Korea	Japan	US	Europe
1963-1971	*39.7*	*48.2*	*28.4*	*16.4*
1972-1980	*27.7*	*22.9*	*17.4*	*12.7*
1981-1990	*16.9*	*14.4**	*12.6**	*13.4**

[*Japan, America and Europe: 1981-1987. Source: Japan, US and Europe; Armstrong et al, *Capitalism Since 1945* (Oxford, 1991), Appendix data A1, A2. South Korea: H W Jang, 'Phases of Capital Accumulation in Korea and Evolution of Government Growth Strategy, 1963-1990', unpublished D Phil thesis (University of Oxford, 1995), Appendix data.]

TRENDS IN PROFIT RATE OF MANUFACTURING INDUSTRY 1963-1990

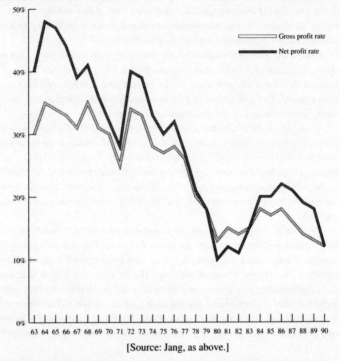

[Source: Jang, as above.]

The Bank of Korea's *Financial Statement Analysis* each year also shows the same tendency:

AVERAGE RATE OF ORDINARY PROFIT TO TOTAL LIABILITIES AND NET WORTH IN MANUFACTURING INDUSTRY

1971-1979	4.42
1980-1989	2.70
1990-1995	2.23

The years 1993-1995 were a short period of economic recovery, relying chiefly on special demands for computer chips and the rising value of the yen. Moreover, the Securities Supervisory Board announcement of 26 March 1996 indicated that many firms employed accounting techniques, which partially hid the declining profit rate. For instance, Dae-il Chemicals turned a loss of 5 billion won into a black-ink (paper profit) of 4.3 billion won. Other companies such as Keukdong Construction Company and

Dongyang Textile Company rigged their profit figures quite legally.[13] The weakness of the 1993-1995 'boom' is shown by the fact that, despite an increase in exports during this period, trade deficits, especially with the US, increased. (The US was South Korea's main sales market until late 1980s.) See the following table:

SOUTH KOREA'S BALANCE OF PAYMENTS WITH THE US AND JAPAN 1981-1996 (£ billions)

Year	Total	w/US	w/Japan
1982	-2.4	0.3	-1.9
1983	-1.7	2.0	-2.8
1984	-1.4	3.6	-3.0
1985	-0.9	4.3	-3.0
1986	3.1	7.3	-5.4
1987	6.3	9.6	-5.2
1988	8.9	8.7	-3.9
1989	0.9	4.7	-4.0
1990	-4.4	2.4	-5.9
1991	-9.7	-0.3	-8.8
1992	-5.2	-0.2	-7.9
1993	-1.6	0.2	-8.5
1994	-6.3	-1.0	-9.9
1995	-10.1	-6.3	-15.6
1996	-20.6	-11.6	-15.7

[Source: Bank of Korea, *Economic Statistics Yearbook*, each year.]

A profitability crisis forced South Korean firms to look to the banks for greater borrowing. By March 1997 the economy had been in recession for 21 months.[14] No previous recession had lasted more than 19 months since the early 1970s, when the official statistics on business cycles began. As a result, the first half of last year saw the rate of bankruptcy (0.22 percent) double that of the previous year (0.10 percent).[15] The number of bankrupt firms increased by 31.1 percent, which meant 48 firms going bankrupt every day. So firms' debt rapidly increased. Already in 1996 the rate of liabilities to net worth in manufacturing industry (317.1 percent) increased by 30.3 percent over that in the previous year (286.8 percent).[16] This figure was almost double the US's (159.7 percent in 1995) and almost four times as big as that of Taiwan (85.7 percent). While the return on net sales of South Korea's manufacturing industry (6.5 percent) was much higher than that of Japan's (3.3

percent) and not very much lower than that of Taiwan's (7.3 percent), the rate of financial expenses to net sales (5.8 percent) was much higher than that of Japan's (1.3 percent in 1995) or that of Taiwan's (2.2 percent). Because of this high debt ratio the rate of net income to net sales was just 1 percent, much lower than the US's 7.9 percent, Japan's 2.9 percent and Taiwan's 5.1 percent. Borrowing is not a practice of manufacturing industry alone. The rate of financial expense to net sales of South Korea's 30 largest *chaebols* (whose net sales in 1996 amounted to 92.1 percent of GDP) has been 5.4 percent on the average for the past ten years, as compared with Japan's 1.8 percent, Taiwan's 2.1 percent and Germany's 0.9 percent.[17]

The insolvency of big firms weakened banks and stock companies. This is a so-called 'compound slump': a combination of industrial crisis and financial crisis. South Korea's six largest nationwide commercial banks' bad debt in 1996 amounted by US standards to 14.3 percent of the total credit, as compared with the US's 1.2 percent (in 1995).[18] Hence the desperate calls for the IMF's relief loan.

Class struggle in 1997

In January 1997 mass strikes exploded against this economic background. They were the first major event in the class struggle since the July-September mass strikes of 1987. The mass strikes in January 1997 were the first political strikes and had a profound impact on workers' consciousness. Trade union organisations were also strengthened. Thanks to the strikes the reputation and the status of the Korea Confederation of Trade Unions (KCTU) was enhanced. This was the most important gain of the mass labour movement since the 1987 mass strikes. On the other hand, the leadership of the Federation of Korean Trade Unions (FKTU), which was transforming itself from a state-controlled bureaucracy into an ordinary right wing trade union bureaucracy, could not stop its base being undermined. It supported the strikes against its will.

The strikes ended up in a victory, humiliating president Kim Young-sam. This plunged him into a grave crisis. He was even forced to send his own son, who had been involved in bribery, to prison. At last the one-party state which has ruled South Korea since 1963 is collapsing. The strikes initially exposed the class nature of established politicians. This was shown by the fact that all the main presidential candidates' popularity fell, according to all the polls taken during and immediately after the strikes. Later it was Kim Dae-jung who was to fish in troubled waters in the presidential election of 18 December. He profited from the class struggle because Kwon Young-gil, leader of the KCTU, was out of the running.

The January 1997 mass strikes proved that workers can resist mass sackings. Unlike the trade union leaders who suggested that they should accept the proposed labour law, ordinary workers consistently opposed it. Now, as the economic crisis deepens and the international financial market increases the pressure, Kim Dae-jung and the bosses are trying to push through the labour law as soon as possible. And trade union leaders are trying to avoid struggles against it under the pretext of 'sharing the suffering'. But pressure from the rank and file is so immense that the union leaders are hesitating to enter what they call a 'Social Agreement' with Kim Dae-jung. The president elect is trying to allure KCTU leaders into the Committee of Labour, Management and Government to achieve what he calls a 'National Agreement', which means bartering structural reform of the *chaebols* in return for the unions' acceptance of massive sackings.

Despite the rise in workers' consciousness and organisation, the January 1997 strikes fell short of ordinary workers' expectations that there would be a definite improvement in their conditions. This demoralised a significant number of militant workers. The fault lay with the KCTU leaders who suddenly retreated to a 'strike every Wednesday' tactic on 18 January 1997, when the strikes showed some signs of escaping their control. The strikes had petered out before the union leaders finally called them off on 28 January under the pretext of the Hanbo *chaebol*'s bankruptcy. But this didn't mean that the workers' movement was put on the defensive after the strikes. Since the rank and file potential and will to fight were not fully unleashed, the ruling class did not dare to launch a full scale counter-offensive.

Individual bosses nonetheless quickly counter-attacked individual militant activists, taking advantage of the rank and file confusion at the union leaders suddenly ending the strikes. This was made possible because company based union leaders, as well as the national bureaucracy of the KCTU, assured their bosses that the target of the strikes was not them but only the government. The KCTU leaders refused to support the economic strikes staged in mid-January by several company based unions belonging to the FKTU, the right wing trade union confederation. In doing so they argued that the January strikes were political strikes and therefore should be confined to the key political demand, ie repealing the labour law which had been rushed through the National Assembly by surprise on Boxing Day of the previous year. Since workers in the FKTU were paid less and worked in worse conditions than those in the KCTU, they tended to support economic demands at the height of more advanced workers' struggles. But, especially in state capitalist countries like South Korea, the political and the economic cannot easily be separated, and yet the reformist union bureaucracy was and is always trying to separate one from the other. For instance, the KCTU leadership refused openly to defend the *Hanchongryon,* the Korea Confederation of Student Councils, when they were witch hunted and arrested *en masse* in August to September 1996 and in June to early November 1997.

Despite the victimisation of rank and file militants, the ruling class was still on the defensive in terms of the balance of class forces across the whole society. In spring 1997 the public hearing on the Hanbo scandal took place. Concern focused on whether Kim Young-sam was personally involved in the corruption scandal. The whole process of the hearing was concentrated on pacifying popular wrath. This would not have been possible without the co-operation of Kim Dae-jung's NCNP (National Congress for New Politics), then the major opposition party. Confronted with a serious challenge from below demanding the president's resignation, however, Kim Young-sam was forced to have his son sent to prison. Student demonstrators shouted on the street, 'Down with Kim Young-sam!' and the popular masses applauded, protesting against riot police brutality. In late May the Democratic Professors' Association demanded in a press conference that Kim resign immediately. Sadly, the KCTU simply kept silent.

It was at the height of students' anti Kim Young-sam protest demonstrations that in early June a man named Lee Seok was beaten to death by student militants who believed he was a police spy. At that time *agents provocateurs* were sent into university campuses to get secret information on wanted *Hanchongryon* leaders.[19] It was regretable that any individual, whether or not he was a secret agent, should have been killed. But this could not justify the regime's sickening hypocrisy. How many people were killed, injured, tortured and imprisoned in protest against the regime's vicious repression? How many people were disabled and killed as industrial accident victims, their deaths ignored by their state? South Korea's rulers supported the massacres in the second Gulf War in 1991 and in Somalia in 1993, respectively, by financing the US army and by sending troops. They were not entitled to condemn violence and to speak of 'humanity' and 'morality'.

The witch hunt which followed the killing threw the student movement on the defensive in an instant. Sadly, the middle class left-populist National Union for Reunification and Democracy (NURD) joined the denunciation of the *Hanchongryon.* The leadership of the KCTU simply kept silent, abstaining on this important political issue. Under the slogan of 'The labour movement going with the people', the populist leaders of the KCTU implicitly agreed with the NURD that it was wrong to demand Kim Young-sam's resignation, speaking of 'judgement through the presidential election', though Kim's term of office still had another nine months to run (until February 1998). Of course, the *Hanchongryon* was (and still is) dominated by supporters of the North Korean regime. So real Marxists in South Korea criticised the Stalinism of the *Hanchongryon* leadership from the perspective of socialism from below and internationalism. But the whole thrust of the opportunist attack on them was oriented in the wrong direction: the critics' argument missed the point of whether they came from reformist, Stalinist or liberal perspectives. As the government's repression on student activists went too far, especially in October when Kia and other car workers were threatening a national strike for job security, the opportunists moved to an equivocal position, juxtaposing defence and criticism of the *Hanchongryon*.

Even after the students' anti-government demonstrations were undermined the crisis of the Kim Young-sam government was far from over. Although there was little agitation by trade union leaders, workplace labour disputes increased from late June. The industrial struggles whose key demand was a job security agreement culminated in the Kia workers' strike in late October. Since the problem of job insecurity became an issue for the whole class as a result of the deepening economic slump, the Kia workers' struggle became a national focus. So the regime organised another witch hunt, in addition to that on student militants, as its own focus for national attention. (In ancient Chinese military tactics this manoeuvre is called 'shouting in the east, striking in the west'.) This was all the more necessary because the popularity of Lee Hoi-chang, the governing New Korea Party's (NKP) candidate, plummeted after it was revealed that his son had evaded military conscription by taking advantage of his father's privileged position. On this pretext Rhee In-je seceded from the NKP and formed the splinter New People's Party (NPP).

The witch hunt was formally directed against Kim Dae-jung. On 8 October a far right magazine supported by the National Security Planning Board (the NSPB, which was the Korean CIA before 1980) organised a 'Discussion for the Inspection of Presidential Candidates' Ideology'. This was televised on all TV channels from 10am until 4pm! The target of the magazine, the *Monthly Korea Forum*, was Kim Dae-jung. The KCTU's candidate, Kwon Young-gil, was completely and deliberately ignored by the establishment's media and so excluded from the discussion. The 'discussion' was *de facto* a McCarthyist hearing. Kim Dae-jung defended himself well in his own way—simply because he was not a left winger. (Western media portrayal of him as a 'centre-left' is sheer nonsense. Before the 1987 mass strikes he was a middle of the road politician but since then has moved rightward, and is now a centre-right ruling class politician. He is now willing to embrace far right politicians like the former head of the Korean CIA, who previously tried to have him killed. Kim is allied to the conservative politicians of the

United Liberal Democrats who serve as his protectors.

So the far right's ideological assault failed in relation to Kim. But the other edge of the far right's knife, which was directed against the left, was not so blunt. Moreover, it was rumoured at that time that the NSPB was digging up a North Korean spy ring and questioning some left activists. This proved true when, on 20 November, the NSPB made an official announcement about its anti-espionage activities. Since both the Stalinist and the reformist left identified the North Korean regime with some kind of socialism, they could not cope effectively with the far right's ideological offensive. This left the workers' movement weakened when it came to deal with the industrial militancy emerging again in October.

In addition to these political weaknesses on the part of the labour movement, the trade union leaders' reformism came to the fore once again. When Kia was first faced with bankruptcy on 15 July 1997, trade union leaders started to talk about 'rescuing Kia'. Did this mean rescuing Kia workers or Kia management? In fact, the KCTU and Kia union leaders supported Kia management in the name of 'keeping the people's corporation afloat', arguing that Kia was not a *chaebol* but only a business group whose ownership was joint stock separate from management. Meanwhile, Kia bosses were sacking non-unionists with tacit approval of union leaders. The leaders of the metal workers' federation criticised Kia union leaders for protecting Kia bosses from the government (whose minister of finance and economy seemed to be considering handing Kia over to Samsung). But they did not criticise the government, merely arguing for building a single industrial union of metal workers in order to bargain collectively around the issue of job security.[20] The overall emphasis of these left wing union leaders was on industrial bargaining. Both the slogans, 'Rescuing Kia as a people's corporation' and 'Industrial bargaining by a single industrial union', failed to meet the aspirations of Kia workers. As early as September, ordinary workers' aspirations for job security were strong enough to force the delegate conference of the KCTU to adopt a resolution for a 'general strike'. But the demand for 'rescuing Kia' precluded other workers' solidarity. How could you appeal to other workers for a sympathetic strike when you yourself were arguing for rescuing your own company? And the demand for 'industrial bargaining' precluded the rank and file initiative and solidarity from non-metal workers.

The Kim Young-sam regime with the official free market ideology did not initially intervene for over three months until 21 October 1997. In the meantime the rulers were busy with quarrels over measures to cope with the bankruptcy of Kia. For instance, when Lee Hoi-chang as presidential candidate visited Kia Motors and promised the workers not to hand Kia over to Samsung, the then minister of finance and economy blamed him for seeking popularity. All the politicians of the ruling class spoke of 'putting Kia under market principles', but they didn't have any clear alternative to state intervention. So Kia was effectively nationalised, put under legal management by the government run Korea Development Bank. Since the National Workers' Mass Meeting was scheduled for 9 November, the government had to 'solve' the Kia problem before the end of October so that the issue might no longer serve as a national focus for workers. Though KCTU leader Kwon Young-gil promised a 'November general strike', he wanted to move as soon as possible to an electoral campaign, making the National Workers' Mass Meeting his most important canvassing forum.

It seemed clear that the 25,000 workers gathering in the National Workers' Mass Meeting didn't expect Kwon Young-gil to be in the running, nor to poll a significant vote. A majority of them seemed to aspire to defeat the governing party's candidate Lee Hoi-chang by voting for Kim Dae-jung. But a minority of them didn't seem to have any illusion in Kim Dae-jung and instead seemed ready to vote for Kwon Young-gil. He argued that voting for him would be a kind of demonstration against mass sackings. Socialists voted for Kwon as an expression of solidarity with this section of workers. In the election Kwon polled sightly over 300,000 votes. Of the whole 550,000 members of the KCTU some 120,000 to 150,000 voted for him, according to the KCTU's own estimate.

After the Kia problem was 'solved' by government intervention in late October, Lee Hoi-chang, the government's candidate, began to rapidly gain support among the ruling class. In addition, in early November the NKP formally broke with the retiring and hated president Kim Young-sam and integrated the smaller opposition Democratic Party into the Grand New Party (GNP). On the other hand, Rhee In-je was reported, to his disadvantage, to have the support of Kim Young-sam. All these facts combined to raise Lee Hoi-chang's popularity. Then, apart from the announcement on the North Korean spy ring mentioned above, the NSPB announced in early December 1997 that a former Kim Dae-jung man, who had defected to North Korea in August, had sent a letter of support to Kim Dae-jung from Pyongyang. A few days later the NSPB made another announcement: it had obtained a video tape of a press conference given by this man in Pyongyang in order to express his support for Kim Dae-jung. Several days later the top secret agency announced that, citing a Christian minister who had visited North Korea, North Korea's ruler Kim Jeong-il had given Kim Dae-jung a slush fund. (A pro Kim Dae-jung weekly news magazine, *Shisa Journal*, disclosed that all these were sheer fabrications made in collaboration with the

North Korean regime in exchange for financial aid and construction contracts!) Finally, on 17 December, the day before the election, the GNP delivered an official statement declaring, 'A red government is not to be allowed to establish in Seoul.'

Crash and the 'IMF era'

It was against the background of the economic crisis that the unprecedented financial crash erupted in South Korea. The financial crash is not the cause but an effect—albeit an important one—of the industrial crisis. But it deepens and exposes the industrial crisis. When the crash was felt in earnest by ordinary people from late November, with the 'coming of the IMF era', many started to argue that the responsibility rested with the government and the *chaebols*. Lee Hoi-chang's election chances were definitively and irrecoverably hit by this anger and panic. The crisis combined with the effects of the January mass strikes to encourage sections of the ruling class to choose Kim Dae-jung as the organiser of a crisis management government, specially charged with getting the workers' movement under control. Hence his victory in the presidential election—the first transfer of power since 1963, from which the present one-party state originated.

But Kim Dae-jung will have little room for manoeuvre, given the pressures from the international financial market. The harsh terms of the IMF deal will mean mass unemployment, severe austerity, economic stagnation, rising prices, absolute poverty and continuing repression. The government's National Statistical Office has recently estimated that this year's unemployment rate will be 5 percent, with the number unemployed rising to one million. But the KCTU has estimated that the rate of unemployment will be 10 percent. At present, at least 4,000 people are being dismissed each day. The domestic interest rate is around 30 percent. Already 100 listed firms face bankruptcy, says a law firm partner.[21] He adds that at least four of the 30 largest *chaebols* are among them—one is in the top ten largest *chaebols,* another is in the top 20. Prices are officially estimated to rise 11.3 percent by the end of this year. Quoting David Ruccio, Chris Harman indicated that '[the various programmes implemented in the different Latin American states] did not end inflation, restore employment or solve balance of payments problems'.[22] Deflationary policies at a time of inflation can result in stagflation. South Korean bosses are now crying, 'Export is the only way out.' This means a rising rate of exploitation for South Korean workers. Already in the years 1993-1995, during the economic 'recovery' fuelled by rising exports (especially computer chips) to the other Asian countries, the rate of exploitation rose from 448 percent, to

466 percent and then to 497 percent.[23]

Furthermore, unlike Kim Young-sam in 1993, president Kim Dae-jung in 1998 will be faced with a strong workers' movement and a revived left, albeit a reformist one. In 1993 there was a political vacuum on the left. Traditional left wingers were demoralised and disoriented by the defeat in the presidential election held at the end of the previous year and by the collapse of the USSR in 1991. In 1993 Kim Young-sam was faced with a very weak bourgeois opposition party without Kim Dae-jung (who was then in Britain). In 1998 Kim Dae-jung will be faced with the former governing party which is a majority in the parliament.

This will mean that Kim Dae-jung will have no choice but to rely on trade union leaders to control the strong workers' movement. He has already established the Committee of Labour, Management and Government in order to tempt them to co-operate with massive sackings. A conservative public opinion poll taken on 9 January 1998 showed that 10.5 percent of the nation opposed the participation of trade union leaders in the committee and that 47.3 percent opposed the sackings. This figure will probably be much higher among workers. So in the delegate conference of the KCTU held on 8-9 January, the overwhelming mood was of opposition to their leaders' participation in the committee. Sadly, nonetheless, the KCTU leadership decided to participate. Hence Kim Dae-jung's success in establishing the committee. But the committee will be fragile because of workers' bitterness and anger.

The KCTU leadership and the reformists in general demand reform of *chaebols* as a precondition for a deal. This is what they call 'Social Agreement' and what Kim Dae-jung calls a 'National Agreement'. Of course, *chaebols* are notoriously greedy diversified capitalist operations—so diversified that they are known as 'octopus' legs'. And as the bosses of the crisis ridden system they are partly responsible, together with the state bureaucracy, for the economic crisis. But the fundamental responsibility lies with the system itself, otherwise why would there be an economic crisis in Europe where there are few equivalents to South Korea's *chaebols*?[24] Why is the US economy's current 'boom' so feeble when there are so few *chaebols*?[25] The real problem with the demand for the reform of *chaebols* is that in the process of 'structural readjusting' the *chaebols* workers are also 'structurally readjusted', ie sacked. So bartering massive sackings for reform of *chaebols* is not what bosses call a 'sharing of sufferings' but an exclusive bearing of suffering by the working class. Since workers are not responsible for the economic crisis, we should not pay the price.

Even if Kim Dae-jung succeeds in concluding a 'National' or 'Social Agreement' with trade union leaders, workers can resist the bosses' attacks that are to come. This will pressure union leaders to question

their loyalty to the agreement, to renegotiate its terms. This is most likely
if the economy does not improve quickly, because the agreement is justified by appealing to the prospect of an economic recovery. (Kim
Dae-jung promised 'to rescue the economy within one and half years'.)
This doesn't mean that workers will not struggle in the next one and half
years. There will be sharp contradictions right from the beginning. In any
case many workers (including the 120,000 to 150,000 belonging to the
KCTU) voted for Kwon Young-gil, not for Kim Dae-jung, without
having any illusion in the possibility of his winning the election. Above
all, many of the workers who voted for Kim Dae-jung did so simply with
the intention of defeating the candidate of the hated governing party. But
initial stimulus can also come from elsewhere, ie from the political crisis
of the Kim Dae-jung government.

The history of class struggle in South Korea has many examples of
political crises for the regime lending an impetus to workers' struggles.
For instance, before the January 1997 strikes, the year 1996 saw Kim
Young-sam surrounded by foes on all sides. From mid-November to
early December 1995 he was confronted with the biggest popular resistance since his inauguration. It opposed Kim Young-sam's protection of
the former military rulers, Chun Du-hwan and Roh Tae-woo, from the
then popular demand for their imprisonment for the military massacre in
Kwangju City in May 1980. Kim Young-sam backed off. This sharpened
the tensions within the regime, formally around the issue of corruption
which is rooted in the close relationship between the state and capital.
The issue of corruption was explosive enough to raise public indigna-
tion, which in turn made the trade union leaders demand collective
bargaining and an end to bosses bribing government officials, politicians
and bankers. Together with the victory in the struggle for the imprisonment of the former military rulers, this contributed to strengthening
workers' wages struggle in summer 1996. The regime counter-attacked
workers as we have seen, by witch hunting *Hanchongryon* student
activists in mid-August 1996. Finally, in December the governing NKP
party planned to push for a lightning introduction of the labour law alien-
ating the opposition NCNP, only to arouse popular resistance in defence
of parliamentary democracy. The result was workers' mass strikes in
January 1997 against the labour law.

The election of Kim Dae-jung as president will mean more tensions
within the ruling class. And while he will never act on behalf of workers,
his political base is different from the traditional governing bloc of the
state bureaucracy, the military and large capitalists (including *chaebols*).
So it will be difficult, if not impossible, for him to reconcile his supporters with these sections of the ruling class. Meanwhile, because of the
deepening economic crisis, the internal ruling class bickerings will take

the form of smoldering feuds around the issue of economic structural reforms.

Of course, given the pressures from the international financial markets represented by the IMF deal Kim Dae-jung will have little room for manoeuvre. So many people, including those on both the reformist and Stalinist left, argue that South Korea has become an 'economic colony' without 'economic sovereignty' under 'the IMF's trusteeship'.[26] Many on the left even explain the crash by talking about the US's conspiracy to take over the South Korean market, the so-called 'New MacArthur Scenario'. But South Korea has its own ruling class with its own methods of capital accumulation free from imperialist oppression. A centre-right magazine has recently disclosed that some of the international financiers who are creditors to South Korea's domestic financial market are in fact Koreans.[27] They are called 'foreign capital with black hair' in the financial market. Their money, disguised as foreign funds, aims chiefly at the merger and aquisition of domestic companies whose stock value has plummeted. The total amount of 'foreign capital with black hair' in the global financial market is estimated to be between $10 billion and $20 billion. So the 'IMF era' will involve a class struggle rather than a Third Worldist national struggle.[28]

The inner conflicts within the ruling class will mean that sooner or later working class struggle will emerge. In the process, the biggest beneficiary on the left will initially be the reformists, given the fact that the revolutionary left is severely repressed by the secret police and alienated from the mainstream labour movement. The International Socialists of South Korea (ISSK) will, however, be able to grow and to begin to implant themselves in the working class movement—if they can find a way in which they can operate in this milieu without being culled by the police.

Notes

1   Interview with the *Chosun Ilbo*, 13 January 1997.
2   Interview with the *Seoul Kyoungje Shinmun*, 1 January 1997.
3   IMF, *World Economic Outlook* (October 1996). Quoted in the *Seoul Kyoungje Shinmun*, 28 February 1997.
4   Quoted in the *Mae-il Kyoungje Shinmun*, 4 February 1997.
5   Quoted in the *Chosun Ilbo*, 5 February 1997.
6   Quoted in the *Chosun Ilbo*, 22 August 1997.
7   Ministry of Finance and Economy, Economic White Paper (Seoul, 1997), p39.
8   The *Chosun Ilbo*, 14 June and 6 October 1997.
9   This is the most recent figure estimated by the Ministry of Finance and Economy, pressured by the American Department of the Treasury. Vice-Secretary Lawrence Sommers argued in a press conference held at the end of last year that South Korea's real external liabilities were $240 billion.
10   Bank of Korea, *Financial Statement Analysis* (Seoul, 1997).
11   Securities Supervisory Board announcement, 26 March 1996.
12   C Harman, *Explaining the Crisis* (Bookmarks, 1984), p115.

13   Securities Supervisory Board announcement, 26 March 1996. Chris Harman had
      earlier indicated such profit overstatements by firms. See C Harman, 'Where is
      Capitalism Going?', *International Socialism* 58 (London, 1993), pp20-22.
14   Bank of Korea announcement, 22 May 1997.
15   Bank of Korea announcement, 24 August 1997.
16   Bank of Korea, *Financial Statement Analysis* (Seoul, 1997).
17   Korea Institute of Finance report, 5 September 1997.
18   Committee for Financial Reform report, 1996.
19   The *Han-kyoreh*, 19 June 1997.
20   Kang Shin-joon, 'How Should Workers Look at the Kia Question?', *Solidarity
      and Practice* 37 (Youngnam Institute of Labour Movement, July 1997). In the
      1980s Alex Callinicos observed a similar division and eclecticism between
      populism and workerism in South Africa. See his *South Africa: Between Reform
      and Revolution* (Bookmarks, 1988), especially pp88-104.
21   *News+* 118, 22 January 1998, p44.
22   C Harman, 'Where is Capitalism Going? (Part Two)', *International Socialism* 60,
      (London, 1993), p116.
23   Seong-jin Jeong, 'Social Structure of Accumulation of South Korean Economy
      and its Collapse', Conference of Progressive Academic Groups (ed), *June 1987
      Democratic Uprisings and Korean Society Ten Years Since* (Seoul, 1997), pp41-
      42. Professor Jeong is a Marxist academic.
24   Some commentators argue that the *chaebol* is not a peculiar form of capitalist
      organisation to be found in South Korea alone. But in South Korea a *chaebol*
      means a large, diversified group of companies which are both owned and
      monolithically managed by its head, his family and his blood relatives, and which
      has grown under the auspices of the government, relying on borrowed capital.
      According to this definition, there are *chaebols* in some other NICs too (like in
      Indonesia, with Suharto family's business group). For a definition closest to this
      see P Jones and Il Sakong, *Government, Business, and Entrepreneurship in
      Economic Development: The Korean Case* (Harvard University Press, 1980).
25   J Geier and A Shawki, 'Contradictions of the "Miracle Economy"', American
      ISO's *International Socialist Review* 2 (Chicago, 1997), pp6-14.
26   For a typically Third Worldist and Stalinist outlook on South Korea's economic
      crisis, see Institute of Democratic Trade Union Movement, *The Great Economic
      Crisis and the IMF's Trusteeship* (Seoul, 1998).
27)   *News+* 118, 22 January 1998, pp20-21. Alex Callinicos, quoting J Petras and M
      Morley, pointed to a similar phenomenon in Latin America. See his article
      'Marxism and Imperialism Today', *International Socialism* 50 (London, 1991),
      p25.
28   Ibid.

Financial crises and the real economy

ROB HOVEMAN

The Asian 'Tiger' economies (South Korea, Taiwan, Hong Kong and Singapore) and the 'Tiger cubs' (Indonesia, Malaysia, Thailand and the Philippines) are in acute crisis. Some are facing a 1930s style collapse of their financial systems and severe economic contraction.

These were the showcases of contemporary capitalism. They boasted phenomenal rates of economic growth over a number of years. For example, South Korea, the biggest of the Tigers, had an average annual growth rate of 8 percent from 1960 through to 1997, making it temporarily the eleventh largest economy in the world and giving it membership of the prestigious Organisation of Economic Cooperation and Development, the OECD.

The Tigers provided a model of economic growth for less developed countries on the basis of export led growth, assisted in many instances by substantial state direction and protection for the domestic economy. Tony Blair visited Singapore, and Peter Mandelson, sponsored by Barclays Bank, visited South Korea before the 1997 election. They both singled out for praise their economic performance and remained utterly silent on the Singaporean and South Korean governments' record of repression, particularly against trade unionists and socialists.

Now the Tigers are in turmoil and the International Monetary Fund (IMF) has been forced to intervene to support loans totalling more than $100 billion in order to try and stave off a collapse that would threaten a worldwide financial and economic crisis. The speed with which the crisis has broken and spread and the depths to which it has so far gone have taken the world's political, business and financial leaders by surprise. Despite the clear signs of financial distress, signalled by the devaluation of most East Asian currencies, Alan Greenspan, chairman of the US Central Bank, the Federal Reserve Board, Michel Camdessus, director general of the IMF, and others were still talking optimistically of this being a short term crisis at the end of September 1997. The crisis, they claimed, would presage timely economic and financial reform, upon which the Tigers would resume their upward path, albeit at a more leisurely and sustainable rate of growth as befits the more mature economies. By January 1998 the mood had changed radically and Greenspan, the arch-fighter against inflation, was warning instead of the dangers of worldwide deflation.

For millions of workers across East Asia the impact of the crisis was already having a profound effect, with layoffs, wage cuts, higher prices for basic foodstuffs and the forced expulsion of large numbers of migrant workers.

To understand why the Tigers have been transformed from miracle economies to basket cases in a matter of months we have to go back to Marx and the theory of capitalist development and crisis that he bequeathed us.[1]

Capital and exploitation

Capitalism is a class system based upon two fundamental divisions: firstly between the ruling class or bourgeoisie on the one hand and the working class or proletariat on the other, and secondly between members of the ruling class as they compete against one another for markets and profit. The ruling class own and/or control the means of production, distribution and exchange whilst the working class have to sell their ability to work (their labour power) to whichever capitalist, if any, can profitably employ them.

Surplus value (put crudely, profit) is then extracted from workers by paying them less in wages than the value they create in the process of production. That is why exploitation lies at the heart of the capitalist system.

The bosses, however, constantly face the threat of competition from other bosses, forcing any boss, if he or she is to remain successful and to avoid takeover or bankruptcy, to try to increase the length and intensity of the working day and to try to minimise the wage paid to the worker. There are limits, however, to how far this process can go, limits set by the physical health of the workers, by their expectations and above all their collective resistance. Limits are also set by the supply of suitable labour. Shortages of labour put the bosses into competition with one another to attract and retain labour, which can mean rises in wages rather than cuts.

The bosses also therefore compete by trying to raise productivity and expand their markets through investment in more and more sophisticated technology. If they can cut the cost of producing certain goods and make those goods more attractive, they will be able to grab a bigger share of the pool of surplus value and therefore a bigger slice of the profit.

Productive capital

Productive capital, which equates broadly to the real economy, refers to the investment of surplus value in the production of commodities for sale, in order to increase the capitalist's surplus value. The capitalist will spend his profits or money borrowed from the banks or raised in the stock markets (M) on buying materials, machines and employing workers (C) to produce goods (P) of higher value than the cost of the original materials, machines and labour. These new goods (C1) are then sold for more than the cost of the labour and the machines (themselves produced by past or 'dead' labour) which produced those goods. This provides the bosses with an increase on their original investment (M1). This is the industrial or productive circuit of capital identified by Marx in the formula $M-C-P-C^1-M^1$.

The increase in value that accrues to the capitalist is derived from the exploitation of the working class employed in the production process. Providing the goods are sold, this surplus value then accrues to the capitalist class as a whole and is divided into profits, interest, dividends and rent.

Money

In a barter economy goods are exchanged by the immeddiate producers directly for other goods that they need or desire. Such exchange will normally be dictated by the relative amounts of labour that were expended in the production of those goods. In a capitalist economy, however, the exchange of goods takes place through the medium of money. Capitalism is a system of generalised commodity production. Goods are not produced for immediate exchange with other goods. They are produced in the hope that there is a market for those goods, a market mediated by money—the universal equivalent which measures the relative value of goods, acts as the means of exchange and also as a store of value. Money therefore represents a claim on the total social production in a society. And labour itself becomes a commodity under capitalism, with the working class having to sell its ability to work to the bosses in return for a wage, a wage that will then be used to purchase shelter, clothing and food.

Money obscures the key role of labour in the production of goods. Capitalists are able to portray themselves as the wealth creators because they accumulate money over time through the exploitation of the working class and use the social power that this money represents to determine what will be invested, who will be employed and at what rate, etc. That wealth represents a social dependency of the working class on the decisions of the tiny minority of bosses. Laughably, bourgeois apologists have claimed the profit that the capitalist class reaps is a reward for their abstention from consumption, a claim that a momentary glimpse at the lifestyles of the rich will immediately refute. The fact is that nothing can be produced without workers working, as any strike demonstrates.

Money also obscures the role of labour in the determination of the relative values of different commodities. The value of commodities is ultimately determined by the amount of labour time that is required on average in the production of those commodities. It is this 'socially necessary labour time' that determines the relative value of goods and ultimately underpins the value of money itself.

However, money also allows a limited freedom in the determination of relative prices. A picture penned in an hour by Picasso may be 'worth' more than a house that involved hundreds and even thousands of hours of labour, because those with large amounts of money may choose to bid up the price of Picasso's works. The general level of prices may rise if the government chooses to print money in excess of the growth of the economy—a phenomenon known as inflation—and relative prices will be distorted by changes in supply and demand. If demand exceeds supply, prices will go up, and if supply exceeds demand, prices will come down.

Far from Marx having ignored the question of supply and demand which has preoccupied bourgeois economists and politicians, he was well aware of their influence on relative prices and indeed on the dynamics of the capitalist economy. Without goods having a use value which gives rise to their purchase by money holders, surplus value cannot be realised through the sale of those goods.

However, the socially necessary labour time involved in the production of goods ultimately provides the only objective measure of value and acts as a gravitational centre around which prices will move. Even more importantly it is the amount of surplus value, as determined by exploitation in the production process, relative to the amount of investment capitalists are required to make through competition which ultimately underpins the rate of profit in the capitalist economy. And it is the rate of profit which ultimately determines the health of the system.

Financial capital

Some capitalists may not have an immediate outlet for their profits. Other capitalists may have ideas for productive investment but not the capital. The emergence of a banking system and a stock exchange can help to match one to the other. This is the financial circuit of capital.

The financial system means that capitalists do not have to depend on the capital they are able to accumulate directly through the sale of goods produced by the companies they own. They can raise money through stock exchanges, where they sell stocks and shares giving stock and shareholders part ownership of the company and more importantly a share of the future profits in the form of a dividend. They may borrow money from the banks in exchange for a commitment to repay the loan together with interest. Or they may borrow money directly from the financial markets by issuing bonds, carrying a similar commitment to repay with interest as applies to bank loans. Governments and government supported institutions have become major issuers of bonds over the last 25 years as they have sought to cover sizeable amounts of their spending through borrowing rather than through taxing the rich. The market in US government bonds is now the largest financial market in the world. The financial system helps to expand the productive forces under capitalism by recycling surplus funds to companies and, indeed, countries where there are more profitable outlets for investment.

To induce capitalists and others to put their money in the banks, the banks have to offer the depositor interest on their deposits, hence providing the possibility of profit without direct investment in production $(M-M^1)$. To obtain the money to pay their depositors the interest on their deposits, the banks must charge a higher rate of interest on their loans and ensure the interest on their loans is repaid. Again this process helps to obscure the underlying nature of the system by apparently allowing the accumulation of wealth without any direct involvement in the production and sale of real goods.

Whilst a banking system is vital for increasing the expansion of capitalism and for sustaining the complex transactions that occur in a sophisticated capitalist economy, it is also a source of vulnerability. Banks typically borrow short, meaning depositors can withdraw their deposits very quickly, and lend long, meaning banks cannot recoup much of their lending in the short term. Banks may be vulnerable therefore to panic withdrawals or changes in sentiment amongst those on whom they depend for deposits and to changes in market conditions which turn some of their loans bad. In the 1930s many US banks were forced to close their doors to those trying to withdraw their deposits because they were afraid they were about to lose their savings as a result of the collapse of the bank. This fear was fuelled by the bankruptcy of indebted companies and other bank failures. But panic withdrawals then threatened to bring about the very collapse the depositors feared.

To reassure depositors and prevent financial panics, the US government and governments elsewhere in the world have sought to reassure depositors since the 1930s that their deposits in commercial and investment banks were guaranteed by the government, either explicitly through legally guaranteed deposit insurance or through an implicit understanding that the government would not allow depositors to lose their money for fear of 'panic contagion'.[2]

Some bourgeois commentators have begun to talk of the 'public/private' nature of the banking system in the aftermath of the Asian crisis. They claim banks have repeatedly and recklessly lent in recent years precipitating financial crises—for example, the Latin American debt crisis in the early 1980s, the US Savings and Loans debacle, the property lending crises of the late 1980s in the UK and US, the Scandinavian banking crisis of the early 1990s, and the Japanese bubble.

They have done so because they know they will always be bailed out if their risky lending goes bad. Such commentators demand greater regulation and transparency in the banking system and more penalties on banks which make risky loans, even allowing them to go bankrupt.[3] But this ignores the competitive pressures which have led banks to demand and get deregulation, which encourages them to make risky loans and it ignores the threat of financial collapse which obliges states to limit the degree to which banks can be allowed to go bankrupt.

States therefore retain an absolutely vital role in providing the necessary support to the financial system to prevent its collapse and with it the collapse of the real economy. However, 'panic' does not explain why banks in general should run into difficulties which then spread panic. The health of the financial circuit of capital ultimately depends on the creation of surplus value through the production of goods for sale. Financial capital merely distributes and redistributes the surplus value created in the process of production. That is why on a world scale financial capital ultimately depends on the health of the productive sector and it is the crisis of profitability in the productive sector that government guarantees to depositors cannot overcome.

Speculation

Nowadays stock exchanges have a much less significant role in raising capital for new investment. Instead they primarily constitute a market for speculation in the values of already existing stocks and shares. If interest rates are low but profits (and therefore dividends) are high or rising, there will be a relative financial gain for speculators who switch their funds out of interest bearing bank deposits and into shares. A rising 'bull' stock market can therefore reflect rising profits in the productive, real economy. However, the history of stock markets shows that markets have always risen far further in a bull market than rising profitability can justify in the long term. Speculators will bet on stocks and shares in part because they expect those shares to rise and by pouring more money into a limited supply of shares their expectations of a rising market becomes self fulfilling. Sooner or later, however, as conditions and sentiments change, the market will experience a 'correction' or a crash. Such a crash can be precipitated by a sudden significant rise in interest rates, making bank deposits more attractive, or a downturn in profits and therefore likely dividend payments, or shocks elsewhere in the system which simply induce a change from an expectation of rising share values to one of falling share values or any combination of these.

Even if City traders are aware that rising financial markets cannot defy the force of gravity forever, they are obliged to keep speculating on continuing rises until the last possible moment. If, for example, a trader bales out some months before a decline actually sets in he will in the short term be left with results far inferior to those who have stayed in. Therefore it is competition for profit which drives up speculative excess just as it is competition for profit which leads to overproduction in the productive sector. The speculator simply hopes there will be a 'bigger fool' who will take his speculative assets off his hands as the market turns from bull to bear and begins to fall.

Stocks and shares constitute a relatively small area of financial speculation today. Just about anything, from tulips to pork belly futures, can become a focus of speculation in capitalism. In terms of value traded the biggest area of speculation today is in the currency markets. A 1993 survey by the Bank of International Settlements reported that on an average day in the rather placid month of April 1992 some $880 billion in currencies changed hands, up from $620 billion in 1989, an increase of only 42 percent—insignificant compared to the doubling between 1986 and 1989. To put that $880 billion in perspective, it means that the currency markets turned over an amount equal to annual US GDP (the value of total production in the US in one year) in about two weeks, and equal to world production in about two months.[4]

Volumes today are much higher even than this. In March 1995 turnover involving US dollars hit $1.29 trillion up from $700 billion in 1989. Only a tiny fraction of these currency deals are directly related to international trade. Whilst speculators in currencies respond to changes in the real economy, they can also, like speculators in the stock market, profoundly exaggerate the trends. And, as we will see, the movement of the values of currencies relative to one another can have a profound and highly destabilising effect on the real economy.

Economic crisis

When the economy is booming and profits are high many bosses will invest to expand production. Any boss who fails to do this will find themselves outdone by those who do take advantage of the economic conditions. However, the surge of unplanned investment will cause costs to rise as shortages of raw materials, machines and workers occur. On the other hand, the prices of the extra commodities that result from the investment will fall as supply to the market begins to exceed demand. With costs rising and prices falling, profits are inevitably squeezed. Profit squeezes send some companies into bankruptcy, cutting investment spending and throwing workers onto the dole, thereby cutting their spending power. An overproduction profit squeeze therefore leads to cuts in spending which further squeezes profits and makes the crisis worse.

This is the boom to bust cycle in which capitalism is plunged into crisis and recession time and again as a result of 'overproduction'. Overproduction is a phenomenon unique to capitalist society. In previous class societies economic crises took the form of a lack of production to meet the needs of the mass of the population. In capitalism crises take the form of a surfeit of goods. Such a surfeit occurs not because of the saturation of the needs of the mass of the population but because the bosses can no longer sell the excess goods at a profit.[5]

Financial crisis

The impact of a profit squeeze in the productive sector will lead to a deterioration in the financial circuit of capital which in turn makes the overall crisis worse. Lending takes place, when lending decisions are not determined by corruption and nepotism, on the calculation that the borrower will be able to pay back the interest on the loan and within a certain time period pay back the loan itself. Lending contributes to the ultimate crisis of overproduction by increasing access to the reserves of capital that might ultimately be invested. When the expected profits, against which the banks' loans were made, fail to materialise, companies fail to make their repayments and the loans go 'bad'. In the worst circumstances the loans may be called in and the company, unable to repay its debts, rendered bankrupt, the company's workers sacked and the company's assets seized and sold off at 'fire sale' prices to recoup some of the lender's money. This widens and deepens the crisis just as the financial system originally broadened and prolonged the boom.

Banks, which constitute some of the major lending institutions, take deposits which they owe to their depositors. These are the bank's 'liabilities'. They then lend money to borrowers. These loans are known as the bank's 'assets'. To provide some security for depositors and some discipline over bank lending, international standards have been established for the ratio that must exist between a bank's capital (the sum of money that is theoretically owned by the bank, raised from its shareholders and the profits it makes on its transactions) and the bank's assets (its lending). When loans go bad, banks eventually have to write the loans off. Writing loans off is in effect a charge against the bank's capital. This reduces the value of the bank's capital. The smaller this sum of capital is, the less the bank can lend. So an increasing level of bad debts reduces bank lending provoking a 'credit crunch'.[6] This further compounds the crisis by cutting credit and reducing spending in the economy. Banks may also begin to call in their loans as they fear borrowers are getting into difficulties. This will have a further depressive effect on the economy. And the banks themselves may get into difficulties as they find themselves unable to repay loans from other banks and as other banks demand higher interest on their loans or refuse to make further loans to loss-making banks altogether.

Speculation and crisis

Problems brought on by overproduction in the productive sector can be made worse by speculative excess. Rapid rises in asset values (the value of existing shares, property, commodities, etc) as a result of speculation can help to induce overproduction. If property rises dramatically in value, property developers will be encouraged to build more property. In the late 1980s in London there was a big increase in the supply of office space. Unplanned and in pursuit of mega-profits, supply swiftly outstripped demand until it was calculated that it would take 25 years for all of the empty office blocks to be filled. As a result of this excess, and with rises in interest rates making borrowing more expensive as the government sought to rein back the excesses of the Lawson Boom, the commercial property bubble burst.

As speculators turn from buying to selling, asset values begin to fall and the banks begin to worry that the collateral that supported their loans is no longer sufficiently valuable. The banks begin to call in their loans before values fall much further but calling in the loans and cutting credit lines then further depress asset values in a vicious downward spiral.

It is important to understand that speculative excess is built into the financial circuit of capital and that the financial circuit of capital is an inevitable aspect of capitalism as a whole. Moreover, although it is important to understand the distinction between the financial and productive circuits of capital, productive capitalists engage in speculation and speculators may invest in production. The attempt by left reformists to isolate the City as the primary cause of, for example, British economic problems poses a false dichotomy. The bosses as a whole are driven by the pursuit of profit wherever they can derive it from and it is the anarchy of competition in the pursuit of profit which afflicts the working class. But we should also note that speculative excess and a subsequent speculative crash need not necessarily be followed by a downturn in the real economy or adversely affect the real economy as a whole.

The 1987 crash

In 1987 a rapid rise in the major world stock markets was reversed when there was a sudden change in speculative sentiment. This resulted from perceived differences between the US and West German governments over what action to take over the enormous twin deficits on the US government budget and its international trade. Western governments feared that 'Black Monday', 19 October 1987, when major stock markets fell by 25 percent, presaged a downturn in the real economy. They feared that the markets were right in their belief that the failure of Western governments to hit on a package to resolve the so called structural imbalances of the US economy and its relationship to its major trading partners would lead sooner or later to economic downturn.

The 1987 crash was indicative of underlying problems in the continued expansion of the real economy in the 1980s, problems demonstrated by the significant, if brief, downturn of the world economy in 1985. However, in response to the crash governments cut taxes and reduced interest rates on central bank lending to commercial banks in order to stimulate spending, investment and speculative confidence. The reaction of Western governments helped to prolong the expansion of the real economy for two more years but encouraged further speculative excesses in property and shares.

The role of the state

The 1987 worldwide stock market crash illustrates three things. Firstly, dramatic financial events like big falls in the stock market do not necessarily precipitate an immediate downturn in the real economy. They are indicative of endemic instabilities in the capitalist system but there is no unqualified and direct connection between 'corrections' to speculative excesses and major changes in the circumstances of the real economy.

Secondly, governments retain a vital role in the well being of the financial sector and have the power to intervene to seek to prop up and try to rectify problems that emerge in this sector. They do so in three ways: firstly by providing deposit insurance to guard against depositor panics and by bailing out major or strategically vital banks with loans; secondly by seeking to follow the 'Keynesian' path of lowering interest rates, cutting taxes or increasing government spending to stimulate the economy; and thirdly, even if they do not pursue the Keynesian prescription the generally much higher levels of government spending prevailing throughout the post-war period up to today will help to limit the effects of the decline in demand that a financial crunch might precipitate—this is the so called 'automatic stabiliser'.

Thirdly, the knowledge of both the financial markets and of governments about the state of and trends in their national economy or, even more so, in the international economy is highly imperfect. This means that financial markets can be prone to wild fluctuations from day to day based on changing sentiments in the face of titbits of information and the herd instinct. And it means government action intended to address fundamental problems can instead make them worse.

Currency crisis

We live in a world of many currencies, not one international currency. States have retained their own currencies in order for the individual state to have some control over its own monetary policy—essentially the interest rate on short term borrowing—and as a symbol of national sovereignty. For about 25 years after the Second World War the relative values of the currencies of the major Western trading nations, their exchange rates, were fixed by the Bretton Woods Agreement. This fixed the values of currencies against the anchor of the dollar, which in turn was fixed to a gold standard. This was a period of relative stability for currency values as international trade grew at a faster rate than the overall growth of Western economies.

However, the fixed exchange rate system broke down at the beginning of the 1970s. The US had been running increasingly large deficits on its balance of payments, an excess of imports over its exports, as a result of the growing competitiveness of West Germany and Japan, and rising US spending on the Vietnam War. Such a balance of payments deficit would normally be rectified by either the state depressing its economy in order to depress imports and boost the focus on exports, or by devaluing the currency which makes imports more expensive and exports cheaper. The US government did not dare to depress its own economy and could not devalue the dollar which was the linchpin of the fixed exchange rate system.

In the end, those holding dollar reserves outside the US lost confidence in the claim that the dollar was as 'good as gold' and tried to cash in their dollars for gold. This forced the US to abandon the gold link, devalue the dollar and eventually abandon support for the Bretton Woods arrangements altogether. The relative decline of the US and the decline of US arms spending was also the major factor behind the end of the post-war long boom.[7]

In 1973 currencies began to float freely against one another. Along with the growing instability of the real economy, which suffered the first major post-war recession in 1974, large fluctuations in exchange rates began to compound the problems. A large and rapid fall in the value of a currency can raise the price of imports dramatically, injecting inflation into the economy. On the other hand, a rapid rise in the currency can see exports priced out of their markets and imports flood in, damaging domestic producers twice over.

The instability in exchange rates was exacerbated by the explosion of speculative capital crossing the international foreign exchanges to make large and quick profits. In the face of this instability governments have three means by which they can seek to influence the exchange rate.

Firstly, they can seek to impose physical controls over the sale and purchase of their currency on the foreign exchanges—exchange controls. However, the currency markets and the IMF increasingly demanded the end of exchange controls so that they would have the freedom to bale out of a currency if they saw economic trouble ahead.

Secondly, particularly with the breakdown of exchange controls, the government can seek to defend a chosen value by buying its own currency with its foreign reserves (accumulations of other currencies held by its central bank). This can be enough to see off the speculators. However, if speculators are determined enough, the price of running down the reserves may prove too high for the government. The central bank will suffer severe losses if the currency is ultimately devalued despite the intervention or it might even face the prospect of running out of reserves altogether, which would entail that the central bank would be unable to provide the foreign exchange to repay foreign debts.

Thirdly, governments can try to iron out fluctuations through raising or lowering interest rates to lure or repel speculative capital. But this will have destabilising consequences for the domestic economy, artificially boosting the economy if they lower interest rates and therefore reduce the cost of borrowing, or depressing the economy if they raise interest rates.

Governments found that they could not live with floating exchange rates and yet they ran into difficulties whenever they tried to re-establish a fixed regime. The vexed question of the exchange rate remained a running sore within the Tory government throughout its 18 years of office.

The Asian Tigers and the Tiger cubs sought to stabilise their exchange rate situation by tying the value of their currencies to the US dollar. Initially this worked well for them as their export sector saw productivity and therefore competitiveness rise more quickly than other exporters and the industries of the economies to which they were primarily exporting.

However, their competitiveness began to be eroded as the dollar rose in value, particularly against the Japanese yen and the Chinese yuan (since renamed the renminbi), which was devalued in 1994 to boost Chinese exports. As cumulative economic problems of overinvestment, declining profitability and declining productivity, growing balance of payments deficits and mounting domestic bad debts began to increase, speculators began to sell East Asian currencies, ultimately forcing the devaluation of all but the Hong Kong dollar. The familiar problems of rising import prices resulting from devaluation, however, almost paled into insignificance compared to the effect devaluation had on the ability of Tiger companies and banks to service their enormous international loans. By simple arithmetic, the halving of the dollar value of a currency doubles the amount that a Tiger company or bank must earn in its own currency to repay the debt. It was in the first instance this loan crisis that was the most visible manifestation of the East Asian economic crisis.

The crisis in East Asia

Overinvestment and overproduction: Although the loans crisis was the most dramatic manifestation of the crisis, the underlying principal factor which brought about the debacle was a classic crisis of overinvestment in the productive economy. Gavyn Davies of Goldman Sachs estimated that the East Asian economies experienced an unprecedented investment rate equivalent of up to 40 percent of their annual production, a rate of investment unprecedented in history. Investment had an annual average growth rate of over 20 percent throughout the 1990s, rising about three times as fast as growth in annual output.[8] The effect of this overinvestment was rising overcapacity across East Asia. Thus *The China Analyst*, a prestigious monthly economic review, estimated in June 1997 that capacity use was running at 70 percent in South Korea and 72 percent in Taiwan while China was running at below 60 percent, suffering in particular from its highly inefficient state sector.[9]

This overinvestment was a classic product of the anarchy of the market and had nothing specifically to do with the favoured targets of the neo-liberal 'new critics' of the Tigers who sought to blame government regulation and direction of investment and an 'immature' financial system which lacked 'transparency'. Much was made in the West of the inefficient use of the high levels of investment, as a result of state direction and 'crony capitalism'.[10] But this ignored firstly that these same economies experienced their very high levels of growth, and earned the universal plaudits of the West, with exactly the same regimes of export oriented state capitalism in place (with the exceptions of Hong Kong and Singapore). The crisis was not essentially a product of state direction, except in the sense that the political and economic structure sustained high levels of investment which were bound to cause a fall in profit rates sooner or later as high levels of investment have always done in the past—just as Marx predicted they would almost 150 years ago.

Overinvestment had a number of consequences which explain more clearly why the crisis has occurred. Firstly, it expanded the supply of, for example, electrical goods, a key motor of economic growth, in excess of the demand for those goods in the key export markets of Europe and the US. East Asia was hit hard, for example, by the collapse in the price of semi-conductors. Secondly, it sucked in manufacturing imports at a faster rate than the growth of exports producing increasingly unsustainable deficits on the balance of payments. Thirdly, there were increasing shortages of skilled and unskilled labour and growing working class expectations and confidence and, particularly in South Korea, trade union organisation and militancy which combined to raise labour costs. Fourthly, the plentiful supply of loans in the Tigers inevitably spilled over into speculative investment in shares and property just as it did in the US, Britain and Japan in the 1980s. For example, the Hong Kong based investment house Peregrine Investments, which collapsed in January 1998, lent $280 million, a quarter of its capital base, to Steady Safe, an Indonesian taxi, bus and ferry firm with close links to the Suharto family, whose assets in January 1998 were estimated by some to be just $4.4 million! Once interest rates rose, the speculative bubble was inevitably punctured, bringing in its wake bankruptcy, bad debt and the exposure of corrupt and illegal practices.

The extraordinary levels of growth witnessed in the East Asian economies would not have been possible without very substantial levels of foreign lending. Western financial institutions clamoured for the freedom to use surplus funds in the West to lend to countries with relatively low levels of surplus funds in return for much higher profits than could be earned in the West. Tiger companies were able to borrow from Western banks at lower levels of interest than domestically, where there was a relative shortage of surplus funds given the investment boom. And with the Tiger currencies pegged to the dollar, there was apparently no risk of falls in the value of the currencies which would make servicing these debts much more expensive. With the prospect of high returns the West was only too willing to lend. The Bank of International Settlements, which monitors the world financial system, reported in June 1997 that 'total net flows to Latin America and Asia in 1996 alone exceeded total flows for the entire 1980s'. Much of this lending was short term, a factor which was to be crucial in the crisis that broke in July 1997.[11]

Devaluation: In the face of worsening economic indicators across the region, the primary focus amongst speculators, foreign lenders and domestic borrowers settled on the Thai economy. Currency speculators who buy currencies which they expect to rise and sell currencies which they expect to fall finally forced the devaluation of the baht on 2 July 1997, after the scale of Thailand's financial crisis was finally made known to the newly appointed central bank director. He concluded it was pointless trying to defend the baht further.

Once the baht had gone, attention turned to other currencies. Now the speculators were joined by domestic borrowers of foreign loans. The latter feared the inevitability of devaluation and a potentially massive increase in the domestic cost of servicing their dollar loans and therefore rushed to convert their holdings of the domestic currency into dollars, pounds, etc.

The sheer weight of this money and the underlying predicament of the Tiger economies meant that it was just a matter of time before other currencies were forced to float with the inevitably dramatic fall in value. The most significant of these devaluations in terms of the size of the economy was the collapse of the South Korean won.

The effect of currency devaluations in certain circumstances should be to stimulate exports and reduce imports. The forced devaluation of the pound in 1992 did have the effect of stimulating exports and is an important factor in the limited recovery of the British economy since then. Exports from the Tigers to the US became anything from 20 to 70 percent cheaper as a result of the devaluations. Imports, on the other hand, became 20 to 70 percent dearer. However, the circumstances of these devaluations were quite different from those of Britain in 1992.

Firstly, unless there was an enormous increase in demand for exports from the Tigers the dollar earnings from exports would still fall rather than rise. There was no reason to suppose that there was a huge untapped demand in the US for the excess capacity of the Tigers, whilst Europe remained largely trapped in slow growth and the Japanese economy was teetering on the brink of a serious recession, if it was not already in one.

Secondly, rising import prices injected inflationary pressure into the economy and would slow down the economy as it became more expensive and therefore difficult to purchase imports vital for economic production. Moreover, as the prices of imports dramatically rose and foreign loans dried up there was every possibility that companies would be unable to purchase imports vital to keeping production for export going.

Thirdly, to try to make their currencies more attractive to speculators and limit the dramatic slide in the currencies, Tiger central banks were forced to raise interest rates dramatically. This made borrowing much less attractive domestically and diverted economic resources to servicing existing debts. Even worse, it was likely to push even more industrial companies into bankruptcy, producing defaults on loans, further cuts in investment, cutting the spending of workers thrown into unemployment and slowing down the economy even further.

Fourthly, higher interest rates were likely to burst the speculative bubble in property provoking bankruptcies across the property sector and defaults on loans. The scale of this speculative excess in turn threatened to produce dramatic falls in bank lending and even banking bankruptcies. By November 1997, for example, 16 bankrupt banks had been shut down by the Indonesian government and there had been a panic run on the Bank of Central Asia as rumours of the death of its owner spread.

Fifthly, and most importantly, the devaluation threatened defaults on many of the loans to the Tigers and reduced very significantly the willingness of foreign lenders to lend and the willingness and ability of domestic borrowers to borrow. Yet the levels of growth in the last 20 years were sustained only on a flow of foreign lending.

Foreign debt: The Latin American debt crisis in the early 1980s was a crisis of Western lending to Latin American governments. The Tiger debt crisis was a crisis of Western and Japanese lending to private banks and companies—it was a crisis first and foremost of the private sector. It was estimated that there were well over $400 billion worth of foreign loans outstanding in the private sector in the most vulnerable Tigers and Tiger cubs—over $200 billion in South Korea, including unreported offshore borrowing by subsidiaries of the *chaebols* (big South Korean conglomerates), $120 billion in Indonesia and another $120 billion between the Philippines, Thailand and Malaysia. Of these loans a very sizeable proportion were extremely short term and due for repayment some time in 1998—for example, South Korea was due to repay $92 billion, Indonesia more than $59 billion. With the devaluation of their domestic currencies making it much more expensive to repay these debts, the IMF rushed to support emergency loans to the distressed economies. The IMF was concerned to avoid major defaults on the loans which could have precipitated a worldwide financial crisis, as Western and Japanese banks were forced to acknowledge enormous losses, and to stave off economic and political collapse in strategically important countries like South Korea and Indonesia.

However, IMF loans come with very significant strings attached. The

IMF is governed first and foremost by the desire to guarantee that indebted economies are able to service and pay back their loans. Their prescription for this is for the government to cut back dramatically on its own spending and to rein back domestic spending generally so that resources are diverted to exports and even more to paying off foreign debts, including the IMF loans themselves. These policies, already inflicted on the working class and peasantry in many countries across Africa and Latin America, inevitably slow down economic growth further and increase mass poverty.

In addition, the IMF urged the closure of insolvent banks, hurting the Tiger governments' supporters, to try to restore confidence in the remaining financial institutions and to open up their financial markets so that Western multinationals could come in and cherry-pick some of the major Tiger companies. Not surprisingly this provoked resistance amongst some members of the Tiger ruling classes and popular opposition from below. The stick that the IMF wielded was that without the IMF loans and its seal of approval the Tigers would be cut off from the international financial markets altogether with even more disastrous consequences for their economies.

In fact the major credit rating agencies downgraded the creditworthiness of the most distressed Tigers, despite the latter reluctantly agreeing to the terms of the IMF loans, to such a level that some Western investment funds became forbidden by their rules to make further loans to these economies. There was little evidence by January 1998 that the IMF intervention had done much, if anything, to restore the confidence of the Western financial markets. This was hardly surprising given the still emerging scale of their indebtedness and their developing economic crisis.

Bourgeois economists were and are radically divided as to what surgery was necessary and what would be most effective. Some supported the general IMF prescription. Others argued that the economic conditions of the Tigers were radically different from those countries subjected to the IMF's 'Structural Adjustment Programmes', the problem being not excessive government spending and debt but excessive private sector debt, 'misdirected' private sector investment and a loss of competitiveness as a result of the dollar peg.[12] Many argued for reform of the financial sector, erroneously believing overinvestment in production and speculative investment to be a product of the structure of the financial system rather than endemic to the capitalist system. But they were divided about what to do about the weakened banks and the massive bad loans they now carry.

Some argued for a process of recapitalisation and state guaranteed loans for the imperilled financial sector in East Asia whilst others prefer a 'big bang' solution, with weak banks being allowed to go to the wall, companies unable to service their loans pushed into bankruptcy, and allowing over-inflated asset values to plunge. In practice, Tiger governments are being forced to vacillate between the two policies, allowing some institutions to collapse whilst trying to prop others up to prevent a spiral of decline.

No one knows just how bad the crisis will ultimately be for the Tigers and the Tiger cubs and the crisis has affected different countries differently. Indonesia suffered the biggest falls in its currency, reflecting the scale of its foreign loans and the weakness of its economic and financial position. The closure of 16 banks at the behest of the IMF in October 1997, far from improving confidence in the Indonesian financial system, prompted a run on other banks with the withdrawal of $2 billion worth of rupiah. In a new IMF agreement concluded in January 1998, President Suharto agreed a wide ranging set of reforms ending the monopoly of a number of large companies owned by members of his family and his political cronies, the ending of subsidies to some sectors of the economy, the cutting of demand to ensure that there would be no economic growth in Indonesia in 1998 and the disbanding of the state organisation which in effect controlled the price and distribution of several staple foods. Indonesia also faced the probable expulsion and repatriation of many Indonesian migrant workers from other East Asian countries and particularly Malaysia. Despite the agreement with the IMF, the prospect of widespread private sector default on many of its foreign loans remained high, along with backsliding by the government as the terms of the deal began to jeopardise the vested interests of sections of the ruling class. Such backsliding and default in turn threatened to trigger further financial crisis. Indonesia is the fourth most populous nation in the world with 200 million inhabitants and controls shipping lanes which are strategically important for the West. Fifty eight percent of the population are under 25. It needs a minimum of 5 percent growth to absorb the extra 2.6 million new workers who come onto the labour market each year. Suharto, a ruthless dictator who came to power over the bodies of 500,000 people, mostly Chinese Communists slaughtered after the coup in 1965, is already threatened by division within the ruling class. The most important threat though, and the threat which above all had the US government turn over its operations room in the White House to the East Asian economic crisis, came from the threat of revolt from an enormous and angry working class.

South Korea is by far the largest of the East Asian economies, formally ranked the eleventh largest economy in the world (since downgraded to twentieth as a result of its devaluation, reflecting the superficiality of these rankings) and a member of the prestigious OECD.

The government has vacillated between propping up bankrupt banks and companies and letting them go to the wall. In January 1997 Hanbo Steel collapsed under $6 billion debts. In March Sammi Steel, Korea's biggest speciality steelmaker, was allowed to fail. In July the largest liquor group, Jinro, and the third largest car maker, Kia, went bust. However, after severe criticism over Kia's failure within the Korean ruling class the government did a U-turn and announced in October 1997 that Kia was to be nationalised. In December 1997 the government announced it would take over two of its weakest banks, Korea First and SeoulBank, and had persuaded Daewoo, one of the biggest *chaebols*, to take over the debt laden Ssangyong Motor and forced Ssangyong creditor banks to share much of the financial burden.[13] Government support for ailing *chaebols* further rattled Korea's creditors and the IMF insisted that any IMF backed loan agreement had to involve the closure of insolvent companies and banks, the break up of protective aspects of the *chaebols*, the opening of Korea's financial markets, giving Western multinationals the chance of cherry-picking profitable companies at fire sale prices, and the passing of laws making it easier to sack workers. Conservative estimates suggested that unemployment could rapidly rise from 2.5 percent to 6 percent. There was every possibility of severe recession and of defaults on private sector foreign loans estimated by some to be more than $200 billion.

Hong Kong, on the other hand, withstood the pressure to devalue the Hong Kong dollar, although at the cost of much higher domestic interest rates. This helped to precipitate a fall of 50 percent in the value of its stock exchange and of 20 percent in the property market. Whether it would be able to hold on was another question, especially if the Chinese government had a change of heart and further devalued the yuan.

As a result of the devaluation of the yuan in 1994, China had experienced a 20 percent increase in its exports in 1997. It had a surplus on its balance of payments of $40.3 billion and foreign exchange reserves of $120 billion. This was a position of strength from which to withstand the hurricane that had blown through the Asian financial markets. However, 40 percent of its exports went to the Asian economies including Japan. In addition China's labour cost competitiveness, though still superior to many of the Tigers' despite the devaluations, had nonetheless been eroded. With the domestic economy stagnant following the tightening of credit in an anti-inflation drive, exports had been the motor of Chinese growth. That growth was bound to fall in 1998 and millions of Chinese workers faced the sack as the government planned to restructure the ailing state industrial sector. The chances of a competitive devaluation later in 1998 remained high despite the protests of China's economic tsar, Zhu Rongji. Such a devaluation was likely to undermine the Hong

Kong dollar and bring further instability to Asia.

Conclusion

The Asian economic crisis was the product of the tendency towards repeated crises in the capitalist economy identified and explained by Marx in his greatest work, *Capital*. The crisis was likely to have depressive effects in the rest of the world. Other 'emerging economies' like Brazil and Russia were likely to be hit by increased competition and a general loss of confidence in the financial markets. Japan, already suffering from seven years of domestic stagnation and facing a severe recession was likely to see its problems compounded as its exports to East Asia plummeted and its banks were hit by defaults on East Asian loans. East Asia had taken well over 30 percent of its exports, 40 percent if China is included. Its banks were the most exposed of the developed countries with some $250 billion of East Asian loans outstanding, and were least able to cope with defaults as a result of the accumulated bad debts generated domestically. Both Europe and the United States were likely to see intensified competition from Tiger exports as a result of the dramatic devaluations.

Whilst government action can ameliorate the financial and economic crisis and limit the possibilities of a dramatic 1930s style collapse, there is no easy solution for the ruling class. None of this means that a global depression is inevitable. But the world economy is probably closer to one than for many years. There is, however, one thing on which the bosses will be united—that it is the working class and the poor whom the bosses will try to make pay the heaviest price for the crisis into which the bosses' system has plunged.

Notes

1   Marx focuses on the process of capitalist exploitation in *Capital* volume 1, on the circuits of capital in volume 2 and on the theory of crisis in volume 3. For the clearest expositions of the basic elements of Marx's economic theory, see P Green, *Introduction to Marxist Economics*, SWP Educational Pamphlet no 4 (London, 1986); A Callinicos, *The Revolutionary Ideas of Karl Marx* (London, 1997), ch 6; and C Harman, *Economics of the Madhouse* (London, 1997), passim.

2   In the 1980s US building societies, the Savings and Loans institutions (S&Ls), incurred massive amounts of bad debt and many were technically unable to pay back their depositors. The federal government was obliged to underwrite deposits up to $100,000 for collapsed S&Ls under legislation originally introduced in the 1930s. The total bill for the US taxpayer was estimated to run to more than $500 billion. See L J White, *The S&L Debacle* (New York, 1991) for a thorough, if by no means Marxist, account of this episode of greed, incompetence and government complicity.

3   See M Wolf for an example of such thinking in 'Why Banks are Dangerous', *Financial Times*, 6 January 1998.

4   D Henwood, *Wall Street* (London and New York, 1997), p45.

5   Marx's theory of economic crisis is rather more complicated and sophisticated than this brief outline. His multi-faceted theory, far superior to anything bourgeois economics has managed over the last 150 years, is to be found through the three volumes of *Capital*. For a useful but needlessly condescending account of his theory (condescending both to Marx and to those who have worked on economic theory within the real Marxist tradition since) see S Clarke, *Marx's Theory of Economic Crisis* (London, 1994). Clarke ultimately fails to see that a fully coherent theory can be extracted from *Capital* and that there is a reason to emphasise the relative importance in analysing crises of Marx's law of the tendency of the rate of profit to fall and its countervailing tendencies. This law, outlined in *Capital* volume 3 (London, 1981), Part Three, refers to longer term trends within capitalism. The boom/bust cycle occurs even when the general trend of world profitability is relatively high. But when the general conditions for profitability deteriorate, as has been the case since the beginning of the 1970s, the boom/bust cycle becomes much more pronounced and particular countries can suffer prolonged periods of stagnation and worse. Since 1970 there have been three severe world recessions, in 1974-1975, in 1979-1981 and in 1990. Since 1990 the Japanese economy, the most successful capitalist economy in the post-war period, and since the early 1990s the major European economies of France and Germany have all been in severe difficulties. We may well now be on the verge of another world recession. For a clear outline of Marx's theory of the tendency of the rate of profit to fall and the countervailing tendencies, see A Callinicos, *The Revolutionary Ideas of Karl Marx* (London 1997), ch 6. For the application of the theory to contemporary capitalism, see the writings of Chris Harman in *Economics of the Madhouse* (London, 1997), 'Where is Capitalism Going?' *International Socialism* 58 and 60, and *Explaining the Crisis* (London, 1983).

6   In Japan banks are allowed to count as part of their capital base 45 percent of the unrealised profits on their shareholdings. In the late 1980s the stock market began to rise rapidly. This boosted the capital base of the banking sector. As their capital base increased banks were able to increase their lending. Some of this lending was ploughed back into the stock market thus further boosting the banks' capital base, thereby allowing yet further lending. Bank lending was also ploughed into property speculation and into expanding real production. This process could not continue indefinitely despite the assumption of almost all bourgeois commentators that it could. With rising interest rates at the end of the 1980s and the emergence of overproduction in the productive sector the bubble burst. As stock markets fell so did the capital base of the banks. The banks were forced to cut back on lending, puncturing the property bubble and saddling the banks with enormous bad debts. In January 1998 the Nikkei Dow index of share values on the Tokyo stock exchange was languishing below 15,000, the cut off point at which Japanese banks would have to start showing losses on their shareholdings. This raised the fear that what had been a virtuous spiral for credit creation in the late 1980s would turn into a vicious deflationary spiral just as the Japanese economy was heading for recession anyway.

7   For much more on the role of arms spending in sustaining the long boom, see M Kidron, *The Permanent Arms Economy*, IS reprint number 2 (London, 1989). For a comprehensive analysis of the long boom and the period of instability that has followed it since the early 1970s, see C Harman, *Explaining the Crisis* (London, 1983).

8   Gavyn Davies quoted in the *Sunday Times*, 11 January 1998.

9   *The China Analyst*, quoted in the *Financial Times*, 20 June 1997.
10   A term coined in the West to describe the fact that loans and other economic
     advantages are granted on the basis of family or political connections with state
     institutions rather than 'impartial' market assessment.
11   BIS quote from the *Jakarta Post*, 18 November 1997.
12   For example Jeffrey Sachs, who had acted as adviser to the Polish government,
     was particularly scathing about the IMF, and even the World Bank's chief
     economist, Joseph Stiglitz, weighed in with criticisms.
13   As reported in the *Financial Times*, 15 January 1998, in the aptly entitled article
     'The Country that Invested its Way into Trouble'.

Class divisions in the gay community

PETER MORGAN

It is becoming increasingly common for some commentators to argue that gay oppression is a thing of the past. *The Economist* said recently, 'The first members of a unique new class are emerging: young gay people who have never feared abuse or assault... They are the front edge of a generation that might be called post-gay: one that may grow up wondering what all the fuss was about'.[1] It went on to suggest that if you look at some parts of the world—the 'cosmopolitan patches of certain Western countries'—then to be gay is glamorous. The media treat gay issues with seriousness: it is more common to see gay characters on television; more and more celebrities have come out of the closet. 'Today if homosexuality were a choice', they argue, 'now would be a great time to choose it.'

Even many writers on gay politics support this rose tinted view of the world. Andrew Sullivan, author of the best selling book *Virtually Normal*, argued recently in the US periodical *The New Republic* that 'gay people [are] already prosperous, independent and on the brink of real integration'.[2] And in the same publication Jonathan Rauch says that we are now moving beyond gay oppression:

> The standard political model sees homosexuals as an oppressed minority who must fight for their liberation through political action. But that model's use- fulness is drawing to a close. It is ceasing to serve the interests of ordinary gay people, who ought to be disengaging from it, even drop it.[3]

The basis for this, according to Rauch, is because gays are now more affluent. He cites recent surveys which allegedly show that the impoverishment of gays compared to the rest of the population is now a thing of the past:

> *As more and more homosexuals come out of hiding, the reality of gay economic and political and educational achievement becomes more evident. And as that happens, gay people who insist they are oppressed will increasingly, and not always unfairly, come off as yuppie whiners, 'victims' with $50,000 incomes and vacations in Europe. They may feel they are oppressed, but they will have a harder and harder time convincing the public.*[4]

But if we look at the position of gays and lesbians in capitalist society today we see that, despite the gains of the last three decades, in particular in the advanced industrialised countries, it is beyond any doubt that oppression continues. Of the 202 countries in the world, in only six countries does the law protect gay men and lesbians against discrimination. Being gay is illegal in 74 of them. To be gay or lesbian in Cuba, for example, means you are likely to be sent to jail. In Bangladesh and Bahrain the official view is that homosexuality does not exist. In Pakistan homosexual behaviour is illegal and is punished by anything from two years to life imprisonment. In Saudi Arabia homosexual acts can be punished with the death penalty. In Australia anti-discrimination laws were passed in 1986 which affect employment, but homosexual relationships are still discriminated against in the areas of immigration, adoption and fostering. It was only in 1994 that homosexuality was legalised in the state of Tasmania. And in the United States although legal protection against discrimination now exists in the states of California, Connecticut, New Jersey, New York, Massachusetts, Vermont and Wisconsin, in six others (Arkansas, Kansas, Texas, Oklahoma, Montana and Nevada) anal/oral sex between people of the same gender is a crime. And, despite the promises from Bill Clinton in 1993, he has failed to reverse the ban on gays and lesbians in the military. Instead he hid behind a compromise 'don't ask, don't tell' policy which led to large numbers of lesbians and gays being driven out of the armed forces.[5]

In Britain discrimination also exists some 30 years after the partial legalisation of male homosexuality. A 1993 Stonewall survey, *Less Equal than Others*, found that 16 percent of respondents faced discrimination at work because of their sexuality, and 48 percent had been harassed. This was supported by an independent report by the Social and Community and Planning Research study, 'Discrimination against Gay Men and Lesbians' (1995), which found that 4 percent had lost their jobs because of their sexuality, 8 percent had been refused promotion and 21 percent had been harassed.[6] The age of consent for gay sex was reduced from 21 to 18 in 1994 but this still discriminates against gay men because the age of consent for heterosexuals is 16. Lesbians and gay men also face discrimination in immigration law, pension benefits, tax and inheritance law, housing and adoption law.

So as we approach the end of the 20th century there is a strange paradox. On the one hand there are those who argue that gay oppression has become so marginal it is virtually a thing of the past. Yet a look around the world shows continuing discrimination, and gay oppression, while it may be ameliorated, remains a structural feature of capitalist society. This article looks at why this contradiction exists. A key reason for the gap between reality and what many writers would have us believe is the differing class positions of the vast majority of gays and lesbians and a thin layer who have been able to find a niche within the system. What I intend to do is to look at what is commonly called 'the gay community' and show that it is a myth to talk as if there is a common interest between all gays and lesbians. In fact lesbians and gays are no more united because of their sexuality than are women, blacks or any other group of the oppressed. Instead there is a division that runs right through the heart of the gay community based on class. And this affects people's experience of oppression, their politics, and their strategy for fighting for liberation.

One mistaken idea that flows from ignoring this class distinction, and regarding more open and visible middle and ruling class gays as representative of a whole community, is that all gays and lesbians have more spending power, or are more affluent than the rest of the working class. But this notion not only mangles reality and obscures the recognition of gay oppression, it also provides ammunition for those who want to resist any moves towards basic equality for gays, let alone liberation.

Gay scene and the pink pound

Over the last few years there has been mounting criticism about the gay scene, the commercialisation of the annual Pride march in London and the growth of the 'pink economy'. Arguments which were once almost completely the preserve of socialists are now being voiced by those who once defended the pink economy from left wing criticism. A book called *Anti-Gay*, edited by Mark Simpson, argues that the scene offers little for the mass of gays and lesbians today. Instead of coming out as gay, he says, we should be in favour of returning to the closet—of escaping from the scene and all that lifestyle entails.[7] Others have argued that the Pride march is now becoming too commercialised. In a particularly powerful article in *Gay Times* Tony Leonard said:

> *The festival has embraced the free-market world of Thatcher and her succes-*
> *sors in a way that was once unimaginable... This year's theme is 'P.R.I.D.E.*
> *What Does It Mean To You?' For the organisers, it seems, the answer is*
> *another five letter word—M.O.N.E.Y... If you thought Pride was about com-*
> *munity, strength through togetherness, fighting against intolerance and*
> *bigotry, and any number of other social, political and spiritual concerns, it's*
> *time to think again. The only hopes, dreams and aspirations we're interested*
> *in here are those involving hard cash.*[8]

Pride, which began as an annual march in London as a demonstration for gay rights and a political statement of resistance, has now
become a major advertising opportunity for some very large and powerful companies—such as Virgin, Budweiser, or United Airlines which,
incidentally, does not extend gay rights to its own workers. The idea
that the event is something that benefits the whole community equally
is a myth—there are important corporate interests involved. So keen
were the organisers of Pride to use the event to generate large quantities of money that they even considered taking out a copyright on the
word 'Pride'—although the proposals were eventually dropped. But
reports of debts and unpaid beills have meant the tensions over Pride
have come to a head, and a new group—called National Pride—have
put forward proposals to run the festival in 1998. We now face the
prospect of two festivals taking place simultaneously in Lodon on the
same weekend as the two groups fight it out.

Some of those who now recognise that the gay scene does not provide
some form of liberation flip over completely from their previous faith in
it. Whether for ironic effect or out of desperation some have even called
for the gay scene to be shut down. Beneath the hyperbole they have
realised how thoroughly the commercial gay scene is permeated by
market values. But the impact of capitalist relations does not stop with
major multinational companies trying to capture the gay market. The
market itself shapes what it is supposed to mean to be gay. The class
divisions that arise from capitalism mean there are both capitalist and
working class gays; there are those with an interest in preserving the
system and those with an interest in overthrowing it. The pink economy,
which countless gay theorists have told us is what holds the gay community together, shows these divisions and antagonisms very sharply.

During the 1980s and 1990s we have seen a growth in the gay scene
in the major cities in the US and to a lesser extent in Britain—Soho in
London and The Village in Manchester are two of the most popular. In
1984 gay bosses formed the Gay Businesses Association whose express

aim was to 'serve the gay business community'. Gary Henshaw, a gay business consultant and co-owner of the Kudos cafe at Charing Cross, said:

> *I am motivated by money and power. There is a certain amount of power and prestige in being recognised as a businessman on the gay scene and I do enjoy that. I happen to be a capitalist in the extreme. I grew up watching Dynasty and I believe that dream that you must struggle forward, you keep expanding and you get bigger until some day I would like to build an empire. Power is very much connected with wealth.*[9]

Gay bosses say they intend to serve the community as a whole— offering gay men and lesbians jobs, opportunities and the like. For them this is one important step on the way towards real liberation. Gary Henshaw describes the good fortune of those who work for him:

> *I think it's a good environment. A lot of young people go and work in a gay business basically to liberate themselves. They've grown up with the problems being gay, suddenly they come out and they work in a gay bar or club and they find people accept them and they have a great time. Then they can go back into the straight environment with total confidence in themselves.*[10]

In fact there is nothing liberating about working for gay bosses or working in a gay bar. Like the rest of the industry the workers are subjected to the same pressures as other workers—forced to work long hours on low pay with very little security. The so called 'community' is there to serve only one interest, that of the gay bourgeoisie and big business. As one employee said who worked for Bass Taverns (a 'gay friendly' pub which sponsors Pride): 'We get paid less per hour after tax than the price we were charging for a pint. Hours would be cut in half without warning. The attitude was, "If you don't like it, fuck off".'[11]

The Gay Business Association was also involved with the organisers of Pride in establishing a 'gay friendly' networking forum whose stated aim is 'to connect the consumer with gay friendly business thereby increasing freedom of choice for the gay consumer and expanding the market'. The launch was at a conference organised by *Marketing Week* magazine called 'Marketing to the Pink Economy' and it said, 'Regardless of your personal opinion, you can no longer afford to ignore the pink economy.' So while the gay bosses may make noises about the need to end discrimination, the need for equality, or the necessity to combat homophobia, they are very much committed to the capitalist system, and they have a material stake in the system on which their profits depend. Gay businessmen identify with the gay community in so far as this is the source of their

income. But politically they may identify with quite right wing ideas—
the market, free enterprise, cuts in public spending, the need to tax
business less and so on.

Gay bosses hold to the idea of the 'gay community' as a way of legit-
imising their activities. This centres on the idea that all gays and lesbians
are in the same boat—that they all suffer discrimination, and so they should
all come together to fight it. Yet such phrases hide the class nature of
oppression, the fact that those at the bottom of society face gay oppression
in a much different form to those at the top. Many on the left accept this
idea of a common gay community. In Britain Peter Tatchell said, 'What
unites lesbian and gay men are our common sexual experiences and our
suffering discrimination as a result of prejudices against our sexuality. A
wealthy gay white man is in much the same boat if he loses his job
because he is gay as a poor black lesbian who loses her job for the same
reasons'.[12] But gay people do not face the same degree of oppression.
Clearly if you are wealthy you can afford the trappings of that lifestyle
that allow you a greater degree of freedom to express your sexuality.

Just a brief look at the lifestyle of those gays who are part of the
ruling class in society shows they live in a world apart from the majority
of the gays and lesbians who are part of the working class. The Advocate,
one of the biggest selling gay magazines in the US, recently featured an
interview with Alan Gilmour. He tells us of the difficulty he had in
coming to terms with his gay sexuality, the way in which he was
accepted in the company after he came out, and how he was able to overcome a certain amount of prejudice. But until 1994 Alan Gilmour was
the vice-chairman of Ford, the second largest car company in the US.
This made him one of the most influential bosses in the US. In 1994 he
resigned from Ford yet he remains on the board of Prudential Insurance,
Dow Chemicals, Detroit Edison, US West and Whirlpool. The interview
in The Advocate tells us that, despite his busy life, he still has time to
oversee the construction of his dream home, a four floor, 13,000 square
foot mansion in Detroit.

Whilst we may have every sympathy with Gilmour's struggle to come to
terms with his sexuality, nevertheless his lifestyle, income and wealth are a
world apart from those workers who are forced to work long hours for low
pay on a Ford production line, many of whom will be gay or lesbian. In
fact, as the article tells us, Alan Gilmour was able to go on many expensive
holidays and business trips which all helped him in coming to terms with
being gay. For most working class people in the US, who since the 1970s
have suffered a decline of wages in real terms of 19 percent, this is a luxury
they are denied. Their main concerns are housing, health, education or
simply having enough food for the kids and keeping warm during winter.

The affluent consumer?

The so called 'pink pound' is used to define a gay lifestyle. The market, or the commercialisation of the 'gay identity', has reached many different aspects of people's lives. This is not something unique to the fight for gay rights. Many other struggles that began as a challenge to the system have been expropriated by the system as the bosses realise the possibility to exploit the market. Now to be gay or lesbian is not simply a statement of sexuality but a statement of lifestyle: it defines what clothes you wear, what magazines you read, what furniture you have, or what vodka you drink. For some, formerly on the left, this is no bad thing. As one writer explained:

> *Political activism, focusing on the injustices and discrimination we face, has a negative aura. In contrast, the pursuit of young-at-heart hedonism offers positive ways of flaunting, rather than bemoaning, gay sexuality. If affirming your sexuality is reduced to a choice between wearing badges, carrying placards, talking about gay oppression and getting arrested, or mincing up and down Old Compton Street, drinking pavement-cafe cappuccino and showing off carefully toned physiques under skin-tight T shirts—the second option is quite simply more fun... If consumerism is the defining characteristic of the gay nineties, and if we have never had it so good, there must be some relationship between hedonism and political gain. It is not necessarily a negative one... Consumerism is not antithetical to political gain, but an integral part of the very process through which these gains are slowly but surely being made.*[13]

The fight to end gay and lesbian oppression, therefore, becomes not one of fighting back against the system, but one of buying into the system, not resistance to the market but the acceptance of the market. It has been accepted by many that most gays and lesbians are an affluent group of consumers, with a disproportionate amount of spending power compared to the rest of the population, who are just dying to rush out and spend all their money on a whole host of consumer goods and products.

Advertising gurus and marketing managers claim this is a discovery they have made in the 1990s. But the image of the well to do gay man goes back to the late 19th century when homosexuality was outlawed. For over a century portrayals of gay men as actors and artists, wealthy and flamboyant individuals have been stock stereotypes. These stereotypes played the pernicious role of suggesting that ordinary people simply could not be gay. That in turn reinforced anti-gay attitudes among workers. The updated version, of gays as yuppies, plays a similar role and has been supported by two recent surveys in the US.

The first was done in 1988 by the Simmons Market Research Bureau which did a survey of eight gay and lesbian newspapers in the US. Its data was one of the original sources for the argument that gays and lesbians are unusually well educated and affluent. Its results found that 59 percent of gays and lesbians had degrees compared to 18 percent of the rest of the population. And 49 percent of gays and lesbians had managerial or professional occupations compared to 15 percent for the rest of the population.[14] This was supported by the Overlooked Opinions survey in 1990 whose results found that gays and lesbians were disproportionately wealthy: 34 percent had incomes over $50,000 (compared to 25 percent for the population as a whole). On the basis of this it was calculated that the 'gay communities' income potential was around $514 billion. *The Wall Street Journal* called it 'a dream market... gay households have characteristics sought by many advertisers. Average annual [gay] household income is $55,430'.[15] Both surveys were used to persuade many major companies to advertise in the gay press in the US which, at the time, was desperately in need of a financial boost. Nor were these surveys confined to the US. In Britain a survey of 1,788 gays and lesbians in 1994 came to the same conclusion—that they were better educated (27 percent having degrees compared to 9 percent in the rest of the population) and lesbians were said to earn on average £3,000 more per year than heterosexual women.[16]

In fact recent evidence suggests that the reliability of these surveys is open to question. Firstly the data they use is highly selective: it's mainly middle class, better educated and more affluent people who reply to these type of questionnaires, so the results are not surprising when you have such a highly selective group. As Lee Badgett says in a recent essay, 'Beyond Biased Samples: Challenging the Myths on the Economic Status of Lesbians and Gay Men':

> *Getting a random sample of gay people in the US is no simple matter. Government agencies and academic statisticians spend a lot of time and money to get representative samples of the US population. Unfortunately few such surveys ask the right questions that would allow a direct comparison of incomes between gays/lesbians/bisexual people and heterosexuals.[17]*

Secondly, it is precisely the class position of middle and upper class gays that allows them them to be out about ther sexuality. Therefore it makes it difficult for any selective sample to be indicative of all gays and lesbians in society. Simply as a result of the numerical preponderence of the working class, most gays and lesbians are likely to come from its ranks. The idea that the majority of working class gays and lesbians can buy into the pink economy is false. For most people this is something that is simply beyond their means. So the idea of a gay lifestyle which apparently transcends class boundaries is, in fact, a particular form of middle class lifestyle. As Peter Weir, one of the contributors to *Anti-Gay*, explains:

> *The gay community represented in Ikea ads, the comfy image of middle class white guys out shopping for furniture, is one that has been identified as the mainstream. It is a lie... The true division in the gay community is between the entrenched, privileged, politically active urban and suburban trend-setters and policy makers, and the mass of people with homosexual urges.*[18]

There is new research which questions the conclusions of both surveys and throws doubts on their reliability. Interviews with over 15,000 voters in the 1992 election in the US found 466 who identified themselves as gay, lesbian or bisexual, and a comparison of their income with that of heterosexual voters revealed that gay voters tended to be in the lower income bracket. This was supported by the 1993 Yankelovich Monitor survey on consumer attitudes which included a question on sexual orientation. What it found was that gay respondents had an average household income of $37,400 and lesbians $34,800—both well below the $55,430 that the other surveys concluded was the average income of gays and lesbians.[19] Lee Badgett concludes that 'all the evidence from better surveys shows that gay people do not earn more than straight people, and two detailed studies even show a more disturbing pattern: lesbian, gay and bisexual people earn less than heterosexual people'.[20]

One of these is a study by Badgett himself when he examined data from the US General Social Survey 1989-1991. He found that gay and bisexual male workers earned 11 to 27 percent less than heterosexual male workers with the same experience, education, occupation and marital status. And he found similar figures for lesbians. Yet even here he adds a note of caution and acknowledges that the reason little is known about the economic effects of sexual orientation is because of the limitations and reliability of the data.[21]

So the idea that all gays and lesbians are affluent is a myth. What has come to represent the stereotypical gay person is, in fact, just a small proportion of all gays and lesbians in society, essentially from the middle and upper class. Working class gays and lesbians are 'excluded' simply because they do not have sufficient purchasing power.

The drift to the right

The repercussions of this debate, particularly in the US, have fuelled a right wing offensive against gay and lesbian rights. For example, in the

US state of Colorado an amendment was passed to the state's constitution which, if enacted, would have removed gays and lesbians from civil rights protection. Amendment 2, as it was known, became the focus for a number of right wing and religious groups to go on the offensive against gays. The Colorado for Family Values group put out a leaflet which said, 'Are homosexuals a disadvantaged minority? You decide! Records show that even now, not only are gays not economically disadvantaged, they're actually one of the most affluent groups in America'.[22] And they quoted a number of figures from gay publications which argued that gays are three times more likely to have a college degree, three times more likely to have a professional or managerial job, and four times more likely to travel overseas than the average American.

Likewise, in his testimony against the Employment Non-discrimination Act of 1994 that passed through the US Congress, Joseph E Broadus argued, 'Homosexual households had an average income of $55,400 compared with a national average of $36,500... This is not a profile of a group in need of special civil rights legislation in order to participate in the economy or to have an opportunity to hold a decent job. It is the profile of an elite'.[23] So the image of the well off affluent gay consumer has now turned full circle and is being used by those intent on denying the fact that gay oppression exists.

Part of the reason why the right wing has felt confident to go on the attack over gay rights is because there has been a retreat by the left in gay politics since the heady days of the Gay Liberation Front (GLF) which emerged following the Stonewall riots of the 1960s. Then there were attempts to link the fight for gay rights with a general fight against capitalism. Today conservative thinking and strategy dominate many of those who write about gay politics, such as Andrew Sullivan, quoted above. They believe the rights of gays and lesbians can be realised within capitalist society through gradual, piecemeal reform. This thinking dominates groups such as Stonewall which remain very much committed to working within the system. Indeed when thousands of young gays and lesbians threatened to break down the doors of the House of Commons and virtually rioted outside following the failure of MPs to vote for an equal age of consent in 1994, Stonewall was one of the first to object and denounce the demonstrators the next day.

Compare this to the fight for gay rights in the 1960s. Then the GLF declared its solidarity with other revolutionary movements of the oppressed and exploited. In some quarters this was reciprocated. Huey Newton of the Black Panthers wrote from his prison cell in 1970 to express his support for the new gay movement. In Britain the GLF organised sit-ins in bars which refused to serve gays, various marches and protests and contingents on demonstrations like the TUC's march against the Tory Industrial Relations Bill. The excitement of the new movement temporarily made up for the lack of any clear idea of how to overcome gay and lesbian oppression. However, the vision of change was very vague and, as the initial enthusiasm waned and the movement had to confront deeper questions—What causes oppression? Can the oppressed unite? and so on—confusion took its toll. Many activists began to see homophobia not as a product of the nuclear family under capitalism but as an inherent attitude in all straights.

Since then the retreat has continued into what is known as 'identity politics', the idea that simply asserting your identity is the way to overcome oppression. But this also leads away from collective struggle. For those who can afford it, it is possible to assert your identity on the gay scene. Clubbing, shopping or fashion become seen as liberating activities, although they are inaccessible to the majority of gays and lesbians. Identity politics therefore centres on expanding the pink economy, making money for gay businessmen, rather than challenging homophobia in the rest of society. Central to identity politics is the idea that the personal is political and the idea of autonomy, that movements against oppression should be separate and distinct, that there should be a gay movement, a women's movement, a black movement.[24]

This approach represents a retreat from class politics, and the idea that the working class could be central to the struggle to end oppression. Today the slogan 'The personal is political', far from leading to collective political action, only leads to the idea that politics based on lifestyle can bring about change. But the problem is that 'personal politics' does not bring about change or challenge the system in which we live. It is not simply a question of alternative lifestyles, or of 'empowerment' through spending, but of challenging the existing order of society which produces and breeds discrimination.

Marxism and gay oppression

The standard attack on the Marxist analysis of gay oppression, as well as the Marxist approach to oppression generally, is that it is economistic. Marxism is discounted, on the one hand, for being unable to explain gay oppression using economic categories and, on the other, for being irrelevant to movements against oppression because gay liberation either does not fit into its strategy for social change or is merely a byproduct of a socialist revolution. For socialists the starting point for gay oppression is that it is rooted in capitalist society, that it serves the interests of the ruling class. Oppression serves to divide and weaken the working class. It sets gays against straights, blacks against whites, men against women, thus dividing one section of the working class against another, promoting inequality and discrimination.

More specifically gay oppression and women's oppression also exist because of the importance of the nuclear family under capitalism. The family is the means by which what Marx called the 'reproduction of labour power' is carried out. This makes it a central institution of capitalist society. In the early days of capitalism whole families were forced to work in factories—and for a while the survival of the working class family as an institution appeared under threat (as both Marx and Engels believed). However, in the late 19th century a concerted attempt was made by the ruling class to consolidate the family as the main unit for the reproduction of labour, from day to day, and one generation to the next. It was at this time that the modern concept of a homosexual identity became articulated. In 1869 the term 'homosexuality' appeared for the first time in an anonymous pamphlet distributed in Germany. This is not to say that homosexuality began at this point—indeed one of the main arguments used against those from the right who argue that homosexuality is somehow 'unnatural' is to point to the fact that this is one form of activity that has existed throughout human civilisation. But it was towards the end of the 19th century that the ruling class moved towards making homosexuality an activity that was illegal. In Britain Section 11 of the 1885 Criminal Law Amendment Act deemed all male homosexual acts short of buggery, whether they be commited in public or private, illegal. And 13 years later the Vagrancy Act of 1898 clamped down on homosexual 'soliciting'. Jeffrey Weeks declares that 'these two enactments represented a singular hardening of the legal situation and were a crucial factor in the determination of modern attitudes'.[25]

The working class family was a cheap way of ensuring the supply of necessary labour. As the nuclear family became more important to capitalism it became increasingly important to portray it as the only way of living. That is why alongside the consolidation of the family came the first laws to criminalise homosexuals. There have been important changes to the family over the last century. Capitalism operates to break down the family—through migration and the demand for greater mobility of labour; through the pressures on the family which have led to increased divorce rates and more single parents; by virtue of the fact that fewer people are marrying in the first place, and more and more children are born out of wedlock. But despite this the family remains the key institution for the reproduction of labour. Working class people still cling to the family as the repository of love and calm from the outside world. Marriage and childbirth are still seen as inevitable for most working class women—even though the reality is still somewhat different. As Lindsey German explains:

One of the most surprising features of the family today is the astonishing tenacity with which most workers cling to it... While these changes have fundamentally altered the families of millions of workers, there is a countervailing tendency for workers to cling to the family, and to attempt to reinforce its supposed traditional values. This is shown by the increased ideological importance of the family and the centrality of the home under late capitalism.[26]

Gay sexuality threatens the ideal image of the present day family firstly because it challenges the family's rationale in the reproduction of labour power, but also because it challenges the ideology of the family. The idea of same sex partners challenges the man-wife relationship essential for the nuclear family. As Tony Cliff says:

So long as the traditional family is an economic unit, for rearing children and satisfying the consumption needs of the adults, homosexuals are bound to be considered deviant: the homosexual male is not seen to fit the man's role as the provider for wife and children, and the homosexual female is not seen to act the role of mother and wife. The contemporary family is not only a prison for those in it, but also enslaves those who do not fit into the sex-role stereotypes connected with it.[27]

This is merely a brief outline of the theory of the family and gay oppression which various Marxists have developed since Marx and Engels themselves. But a number of key features of it are worth stressing. First, Marxism explains how gay oppression is structured into capitalism. It is not simply a consequence of reactionary ideas, rather those ideas rest on the way we are forced to live in capitalist society. The driving force of capitalist society, and its central contradiction, is exploitation. But the way capitalism has developed historically has given rise to forms of oppression which are so firmly built into capitalism they cannot just be reformed away. Gay theorists used to denigrate Marxism for downgrading gay oppression by accounting for it as a byproduct of class exploitation. Instead, they argued, gay oppression is rooted in a permanent antagonism between gays and straights. Some of them even argued such heterosexism was the root of every other oppression and the division of society into classes. Interestingly many of the same people have now interpreted partial advances for gays within capitalism as a sign that gay oppression, which they once thought immutable, can be swept away by the extension of gay business, just pulling yourself together, and quietly lobbying for changes in the law.

The second point about the Marxist theory of gay oppression is not only that it accounts for the oppression itself, but also it explains why mistaken ideas, like the notion that we are living in a post-gay world, can have such a hold. Understanding the class divisions in society is not only key to explaining oppression. It also reveals the class basis of other theories of oppression—how the advantages the middle classes enjoy in society, and the contradictory position of middle class gays, enable them to project their own experiences and class interests as strategies for gays as a whole.

The centrality of class

The history of the struggle against gay oppression is bound up with the history of class struggle and of socialism. And whenever the working class fights back class divisions become more apparent. This was something clearly understood by the Russian socialist Alexandra Kollontai when she argued why you cannot have unity between women of different classes in the fight for women's liberation. The same is equally applicable to gays: 'If in certain circumstances the short term tasks of women of all classes coincide, the final aims of the two camps, which in the long term determine the direction of the movement and the tactics to be used, differ sharply'.[28] Put simply, class interests divide the oppressed—and working class gays have more to gain from fighting alongside other working class people than they do from uniting with ruling class sections of the gay community who have a completely different agenda. Most of the time the divisions inside the working class seem all too powerful— between gays and straights, blacks and whites, men and women. Yet whenever workers struggle, this division breaks down. This was clearly seen during the days of the Russian Revolution of 1917 when workers took power for the first time. In so doing many reactionary ideas broke down.

In December 1917, just two months after the revolution, the Bolsheviks abolished all laws against homosexuality. At the same time abortion on demand was made legal, divorce by request was granted and the age of consent laws were repealed. As Lauristen and Thorstad state:

The sweeping reforms in sex-related matters that were an immediate byproduct of the Russian Revolution ushered in a new atmosphere of sexual freedom. The atmosphere, which gave an impetus to the sexual reform movement in Western Europe and America, was consciously extended to include homosexuality. 'It was necessary, it was said, to take down the walls which separated the homosexuals from the rest of society'... This attitude was generally shared by the rest of the population. The official Soviet attitude under the Bolsheviks was that homosexuality did nobody any harm...[29]

In just two months at the beginning of the century in 1917, the Bolsheviks achieved more than was done in decades elsewhere. The gains by gays and lesbians brought about by the revolution were greater than has been achieved in many Western countries since, although the revolutionary gains were reversed under Stalin.

Today the opportunity to put class back at the heart of gay politics is greater than it has been for many years. Over the last few years we have seen a change in attitudes towards gays and lesbians—now it is undoubtedly true that the majority of working class people reject discrimination. For example, the percentage of people who say that 'homosexual men and lesbians should have the same rights under the law as the rest of the population' has increased from 65 percent in 1991 to 74 percent in 1995. The percentage of those who believe that homosexual relationships between consenting adults should be legal has gone up from 58 percent in 1977 to 74 percent in 1993. And even responses on the one issue that is often used to whip up anti-gay prejudice—the question of whether a homosexual person should be a school teacher—show that, while in 1983 the majority view was that it was *not* acceptable (53 percent), by 1993 the majority view was that it *was* acceptable (55 percent).[30]

For years gays and lesbians have suffered attacks from the Tories, from the introduction of Clause 28 to the continued ban on gays and lesbians in the military. So the election of a government that not only promised greater tolerance but also had the first openly gay MP in the cabinet has brought a renewed sense of optimism. But Tony Blair has shown himself to be absolutely committed to the idea of the nuclear family, not just in terms of photo opportunities, but ideologically. The nuclear family plays a crucial role in his vision of a 'New Britain'. The attacks on health, education and single parents is all about shifting the burden onto the family.

And no matter what the liberal credentials of New Labour over sexuality, a glance across the world shows how there can be sudden upsurges of homophobia as capitalism is thrown into crisis and right wing forces seek to build out of people's despair. Gay oppression continues, albeit at a lower level than in the 1950s. That in itself wrecks people's lives and, given the efforts of groups from the Christian Coalition in the US to Le Pen's National Front in France, it would be foolish to imagine it will always stay at relatively lower levels.

At the same time alternatives to Marxism are in crisis. The gay movement, as any sort of radical coherent force, collapsed into the reformism of the Labour left in the 1980s. That has been followed by an even more stark collapse of its ideas. No sooner had identity politics and the tactics of groups like Queer Nation in the US and OutRage! in Britain become the orthodoxy among radicalised lesbians and gays than the theorists of the gay movement abandoned the notion that there was really anything to fight against. None of this means that gays and lesbians will automatically look towards revolutionary socialism as a way to fight oppression. Many hold out hopes for reform within the system. But that does not have the radical gloss enjoyed by the self-appointed gay leaders of the last two decades. Consequently, Marxism can find a ready audience among gays and lesbians who are sick of being told to emulate an impossible middle class lifestyle and who want to see the banner of gay liberation firmly on the battlefield in the sharp social conflicts that lie ahead.

Notes

1   From 'Now for a Question about Queer Culture', *The Economist*, 12 July 1997.
2   A Sullivan, 'The Politics of Homosexuality', in *The New Republic*, 10 May 1993, p36.
3   J Rauch, 'Beyond Oppression', in *The New Republic*, 10 May 1993, p18
4   Ibid, p23.
5   Figures taken from C Spencer, *Homosexuality: A History* (Fourth Estate, 1995).
6   'Discrimination in the Workplace', Stonewall Factsheet, 1996.
7   M Simpson (ed), *Anti-Gay* (London 1996).
8   T Leonard, 'Give Us Back Our Pride', in *Gay Times*, June 1997, p37.
9   Quoted from N Field, *Over the Rainbow* (Pluto, 1995), p78.
10 Ibid, p80.
11 Quoted in T Leonard, op cit, p38.
12 P Tatchell, *Gay Times*, August 1993.
13 S Edge, 'The Nineties So Far', *Gay Times*, February 1996, pp18-24.
14 A Gluckman and B Reed, 'The Gay Marketing Moment', in A Gluckman and B Reed, *Homo Economics* (Routledge, 1997).
15 From M Badgett, 'Beyond Biased Samples', in A Gluckman and B Reed, op cit, p65.
16 From the *Pink Paper*, 12 August 1994.
17 M Badgett, op cit, p68.
18 P Weir in M Simpson (ed),op cit, p32.
19 Figures from M Badgett, op cit, p68.
20 Ibid, p66.
21 M Badgett, 'The Wage Effect of Sexual Orientation Discrimination', in *Industrial and Labor Relations Review*, vol 48, no 4 (July 1995).
22 M Badgett, 'Beyond Biased Samples', op cit, p65.
23 Ibid, p65.
24 See S Smith, 'Mistaken Identity', *International Socialism* 62, Spring 1994, for a description and analysis of identity politics.
25 J Weeks, *Coming Out* (London, 1990), p15.
26 L German, *Sex, Class and Socialism* (London, 1989), pp44-45.
27 T Cliff, *Class Struggle and Women's Liberation* (Bookmarks, 1984), p223.
28 A Kollontai, 'The Social Basis of the Woman Question', in A Holt, *Selected Writings of Alexandra Kollontai* (London, 1977), p59.
29 J Lauristen and D Thorstad, *The Early Homosexual Rights Movement (1864-1935)* (New York, 1974), p63.
30 All figures quoted from Stonewall Factsheet, 'Public Opinion on Gay and Lesbian Rights'.

The secret of the dialectic

A review of John Rees, *The Algebra of Revolution: the Dialectic and the Classical Marxist Tradition* (Humanities Press, 1998), hardback £36.95; special paperback edition £10.95 from Bookmarks

ALEX CALLINICOS

Marx on several occasions promised that, once he had finished *Capital*, he would write a simple explanation of 'the dialectic'. In the event, of course, he never completed *Capital*, and so never got round to explaining dialectics. We have been suffering from this gap in Marxist literature ever since. Various Stalinist textbooks on what Edward Thompson called 'diabolical and hysterical materialism' certainly did nothing to fill it, since they treated the subject as a set of formal 'laws' which could be learned by rote and applied just as mechanically.

It is not true that nothing of value has been written on the subject. Georg Lukacs' *History and Class Consciousness* (1923) is one of the classics of Marxism. But the book is a series of essays which pursues several connected themes in an often difficult philosophical language: one can learn a great deal from Lukacs, but doing so requires (as we shall see below) a labour of interpretation and criticism. Moreover, assessing the significance of *History and Class Consciousness* involves an engagement with the debates—provoked especially by the writings of the French Communist theorist Louis Althusser—about the relationship between Marx's thought and that of the great German philosopher Hegel, the modern author of the dialectic.

It is no wonder, then, that anyone in the business of defending Marxism constantly encounters the plea for a simple guide for the perplexed through the obscurities of the dialectic. John Rees's new book, *The Algebra of Revolution*, is therefore an answer to a prayer. Written from the standpoint of Lukacs' 'Hegelian Marxism', it provides a clear and accessible account of the dialectic which succeeds in offering the reader an easy way into the subject and at the same time treats difficult and controversial issues with the depth and rigour they require.

As John stresses, the fundamental issue involved in the dialectic is not an obscure or complicated one. It is that of understanding a social world which presents itself—in the mass media, for example, and bourgeois social science—as a chaotic collection of fragments. Doing so requires, as Marx insisted, distinguishing between the surface appearance of things and their underlying reality, or essence. But this essence is precisely not a mere aggregate of unconnected happenings but a totality. 'The true is the whole,' Hegel wrote.[1] Things and events only become comprehensible when set in the context of the web of relationships that bind them together into a single interconnected whole.

This totality, however, is a contradictory one. The essence of dialectical thinking consists in the recognition that antagonism, conflict and struggle are not a secondary aspect of reality which can be removed through a bit of social engineering or the decision of rival classes to fall in love and become 'partners'. 'Contradiction is at the root of all movement and life, and it is only in so far as it contains a contradiction that anything moves and has impulse and activity,' says Hegel.[2] He understood this thesis primarily in terms of the contradictions which develop within concepts: the evolution of nature and human history are an expression of this conceptual dialectic.

For Marx, however, the main contradictions do not exist in thought, but constitute the very nature of social reality. These contradictions are to be located in the tendency of the prevailing social relations of production to become fetters on the further expansion of the productive forces and in the class struggle which develops, within the framework of this conflict, between exploiters and exploited. The contradictions between the forces and relations of production and between classes are the driving forces of social transformation. Dialectical thinking thus sees reality as inherently historical, as a process of constant movement in which existing forms are destroyed by their internal flaws and replaced by new ones.

Marx summed up this view of the dialectic in his afterword to the second German edition of *Capital* volume I:

In its rational form it is a scandal and an abomination to the bourgeoisie and its doctrinaire spokesmen, because it includes in its positive understanding of what exists a simultaneous recognition of its negation, its inevitable destruction; because it regards every historically developed form as being in a fluid state, in motion, and therefore grasps its transient aspect as well; and because it does not let itself be impressed by anything, being in its very essence critical and revolutionary.[3]

The dialectic thus understood is essentially the method with which Marxism as an intellectual and political tradition seeks to analyse the social world.

One might say then: every science has its own method, so what's so special about the dialectic? There are two reasons why the dialectic should be a special topic of philosophical reflection. First, it operates in an antithetical manner to the methods prevailing in the conventional social sciences. These, whether in the form of traditional empiricism or supposedly radical postmodernism, basically accept the fragmented appearance of the social world and its correlate within the academy, the pulling apart of theoretical understanding into specialised 'disciplines'.

This resistance to the dialectic finds expression within the left itself—thus the Italian philosopher Lucio Colletti, during a Marxist phase in the 1960s and 1970s, made a number of attacks on the dialectic.[4] More recently, the short lived school of analytical Marxists, who self consciously set out to rewrite Marxism to conform with the canons of mainstream social science, were similarly hostile. One of them, John Roemer, called the dialectic 'the yoga of Marxism'.[5] Interestingly, this hostility to the dialectic helped take both Colletti and the analytical Marxists away from the classical revolutionary tradition. In the face of such resistance, it is constantly necessary to clarify the nature of the dialectical method and to defend it against attacks and distortions.

Secondly, there is the question of whether the dialectical method can be used to study the physical as well as the social world. Friedrich Engels in his posthumously published *Dialectics of Nature* argued emphatically that it could. Scientific breakthroughs such as Darwin's theory of evolution by natural selection were only intelligible against the background of a dialectical understanding of nature, according to which all processes were governed by certain universal laws (the transformation of quantity into quality, the unity and interpenetration of opposites, and the negation of the negation). Engels' universal theory of dialectics (which had been developed with Marx's knowledge and support) was then vulgarised in the construction of the Stalinist ideology of Marxism-Leninism and used to justify the suppression of genetic biology in the USSR during the 1940s. This led many later revolutionary Marxists influenced by Lukacs to react by rejecting the idea of a dialectic of nature altogether (though Lukacs himself never explicitly denied that nature was dialectical). But this remains an enormously controversial issue among Marxist philosophers.

John Rees negotiates the disputed territory of the dialectic with great skill and aplomb. His presentation is primarily historical. Thus John takes us through Hegel's initial formulation of the dialectic; its transformation by Marx and Engels; the presence of dialectical themes in the great debates within the Second International involving notably Kautsky, Luxemburg and Plekhanov; the intimate relationship between Lenin's philosophy and his political practice; the Hegelian Marxism of Lukacs and Gramsci; and Trotsky's writings on the dialectic. The treatment of these subjects is scholarly and comprehensive, but written in straightforward prose and illustrated with examples usually taken from politics and history rather than the kind of banal and sometimes misleading physical cases (kettles boiling and acorns growing into oaks) traditional in expositions of the dialectic.

Perhaps the best thing in the book is John's discussion of the most controversial subject of all, the relationship between the Hegelian and the Marxist dialectic, in chapter 2. Engels distinguished between Hegel's dialectical method and his idealist system: the first could be taken over by materialists while the second was dropped. But it has never been clear to what extent method and system could be separated without the transformation of the structures of the dialectic itself.[6] John handles this difficulty sensitively. He stresses the continuities between Marx and Hegel—the former's debt to the latter's dialectical thinking, which was itself impregnated with all the contradictions of the epoch of the French Revolution. But he also brings out the differences between them. Hegel believes that all contradictions can ultimately be resolved in the self identity of Absolute Spirit, which knows the entirity of human history as the process of its own development. For Marx, however, contradictions cannot be dissolved in thought: they are overcome through real historical crises and struggles in which old social forms are either conserved, to the detriment of human progress, or overthrown through collective action.

John cites a key passage from *Theories of Surplus Value* where Marx attacks John Stuart Mill for assuming the identity of supply and demand, production and consumption, and therefore asserting the impossibility of crises. 'Here…the unity of these two phases, which does exist and which forcibly asserts itself in crises, must be seen as opposed to the *separation* and *antagonism* of these two phases, separation and antagonism which exist just as much, and are moreover typical of bourgeois production.' In fact, however:

> …the unity of the two phases…is essentially just as much separation of these two phases, their becoming independent of each other. Since, however, they belong together the independence of the two correlated aspects can only **show itself**, forcibly, as a destructive process. It is just the **crisis** in which they assert their unity, the unity of different aspects.[7]

In other words, production and consumption are not immediately identical with one another, as bourgeois economists claim when they assert that supply generates its own demand. They are 'different aspects' of a *contradictory* whole. The 'unity' of production and consumption finds expression in their antagonism, the fact that commodity producers cannot automatically find markets for their goods, and therefore the real interdependence of production and consumption 'forcibly asserts itself in crises', when commodities go unsold in huge numbers.

Marx sums up the methodological difference between himself and Mill thus: 'Where the economic relation—and therefore the categories expressing it—includes contradictions, opposites and likewise the unity of opposites, he emphasises the aspect of the *unity* of the contradictions and denies the *contradictions*. He transforms the unity of opposites into the direct identity of opposites'.[8] One might then say that Hegel's idealism, for all the depth of the specific analyses he offers and the suggestive character of many of his general formulations, finds expression in a tendency to resolve contradictions into 'the direct identity of opposites'. He has quite a realistic insight into the social conflict and economic instability inherent in modern 'civil society', but he thinks that they can be harmonised, in the first instance through the structures of the liberal state, but ultimately in the self knowledge of Absolute Spirit. For Marx, however, the opposites are different from each other, even if they are caught up together, and indeed defined by their conflictual unity. Capital and labour are not the same, even if neither could exist without the other: their contradictory relationship can only be overcome through a social transformation whose tendency is to abolish this relationship, not to transfigure it intellectually.

The difference between Marx's and Hegel's dialectics is brought out by their approaches to a key dialectical category, the negation of the negation. For Hegel the negation of the negation is the culmination of every dialectical process, the point at which contradictions are cancelled and differences resumed into the harmony of the Absolute. This outcome is inherent in the process from the start: Hegel repeatedly says that the dialectic describes a circle, since its conclusion develops from and justifies its beginning. In this sense his philosophy is teleological: the meaning of individual stages in the dialectical process ultimately derives from their contribution to achieving its goal, which has been present from the beginning (*telos* is the Greek for goal). Thus human action through what Hegel calls 'the cunning of reason' serves unconsciously to bring about the purpose implicit in all history of bringing Absolute Spirit to self consciousness.

John brings out very well how Marx's use of the negation of the negation, for example in the famous chapter on 'The Historical Tendency of Capital Accumulation' in *Capital* volume I, differs from Hegel's:

This conception of the negation of the negation needs to be handled carefully, because it is one of the concepts that underwent a complete transformation in its passage from Hegel's system to Marx's. In Hegel, it was the mechanism for reconciling thought with existing reality, for restoring reality unchanged at the end of the dialectical process... Marx's dialectic opens up the possibility of real material change, a real alteration in the mode of production. And although a crisis in society and the emergence of a class that can resolve it may arise 'with the inexorability of a natural law', the successful resolution of that crisis is not predetermined. Precisely because real social progress is at stake, precisely because this involves real classes fighting for the leadership of society, the outcome is not a foregone conclusion, not an inevitability.[9]

The same chapter also contains an excellent discussion of Marx's method in *Capital*. Lenin writes in his *Philosophical Notebooks*, 'If Marx did not leave behind him a "Logic" (with a capital letter), he did leave the *logic* of *Capital,* and this ought to be utilised to the full in this question'.[10] *Capital* is indeed the richest source that we have for seeing the dialectical method at work but, like any complex theoretical text, it is open to misinterpretation. John takes on the ideas of certain ultra-Hegelian Marxists who argue that Marx deduced the concrete structure of the capitalist mode of production from the concept of capital itself. Thus he cites Tony Smith's claim: 'If reasoning can establish a systematic connection between two categories, say "capital" and "exploitation", this is equivalent to showing that one sort of structure (that captured by the category "capital") is necessarily connected with another (that captured by the category "exploitation")'.[11] There are other examples of this kind of approach—for example, the German 'capital-logic' school. At worst this substitutes dialectical wordplay and scholastic commentary for the analysis of concrete social formations; at best it has a tendency to reduce Marx's method to a purely conceptual dialectic.

John rightly insists, 'We cannot treat the book [*Capital*] as if it were simply a progression of self generating categories'.[12] Marx does indeed develop a complex set of concepts, but his aim is to reconstruct in thought the actual historical processes and structural tendencies through which capitalist societies were formed and continue to reproduce themselves. The starting point of his analysis is capitalist society as a concrete historical reality. This is, he says, 'the point of departure in reality and hence also the point of departure for observation and conception'. It is true that, because of the complexity of the capitalist mode of production and the manner in which the surface appearance of bourgeois society conceals its underlying structure, a set of abstract concepts—value, use value, surplus value, etc—have to be formulated in order to identify the nature of this structure. Hence Marx adopts what he calls 'the method of rising from the abstract to the concrete'—of making these abstract concepts the starting point of his attempt to reconstruct the dynamic of the capitalist mode in all its complexity. He nevertheless insists that this method is 'only the way in which thought appropriates the concrete, reproduces it as the concrete in the mind'.[13]

Interpretations of *Capital* which treat it as a series of conceptual deductions often draw support from passages in the *Grundrisse,* the first rough draft of that work, where Marx does indeed sometimes seem to argue that this or that feature of the capitalist economy is somehow contained in the concept of capital. But the *Grundrisse* represents precisely the first of a series of manuscripts written in the decade 1857-1867 during which Marx developed and refined his theory of capitalism. One of the main changes he makes in the course of this process comes in the text known as the *1861-3 Manuscript* (from which *Theories of Surplus Value* is drawn). Here he argues that the abstract concepts by means of which he identifies the basic features of the capitalist mode of production—the theory of value and surplus value outlined in the first two parts of *Capital* volume I—have to be connected to concrete descriptions of actual economies 'through a number of intermediary stages'.[14] This account of his method is incompatible with the idea—central to Hegel's idealism—that concepts can somehow generate their own content. As John puts it, 'Marx and Engels rely on a constant interaction between the dialectic of categories, which does develop according to different principles from the dialectical development of society, but which takes the latter as their constant and unavoidable points of reference'.[15]

There are many other valuable discussions in *The Algebra of Revolution*. But, rather than spend too long summarising what readers should discover for themselves, let me, before concluding, make two more critical points. First of all, as I have already mentioned, the book presents dialectics through a discussion of major thinkers in chronological order. Particular themes are treated in depth in the context of a particular individual's thought. This generally works well, with one major exception, namely that of the dialectic of nature. John only treats this topic very briefly in the course of his discussion of Trotsky's *Philosophical Notebooks* in chapter 6. Here he offers some good reasons for accepting that there is a dialectic of nature, but he doesn't really explore the matter in much depth. This is a pity, since this is such a large and controversial topic as to require quite extensive discussion in a book that claims (except in this case, with justification) to be offering a comprehensive treatment of the dialectic.

An example of the kind of issue such a treatment would have to address is the status of Engels' famous laws of the dialectic. One of Trotskys most intriguing suggestions is that '*the fundamental law of dialectics is the conversion of quantity into quality,* for it gives [us] the general formula of all evolutionary processes—of nature as well as of society'. He goes on to argue, 'The principle of the transition of quantity into quality has universal significance, in so far as we view the entire universe—without any exception—as a product of formation and transformation and not as the fruit of conscious creation'.[16] This claim has much to be said for it. A number of developments in the physical sciences—for example, the emergence of chaos theory, which seeks to identify the patterns at work in the apparently random behaviour of complex systems—have lent support to a conception of nature as a historically evolving whole driven by a series of qualitative transformations operative at different levels.[17]

But in what sense is the principle of the transformation of quantity into quality a *law*? Scientific laws typically explain specific phenomena in the world by identifying the real mechanisms responsible for them.[18] Thus Marx's law of the tendency of the rate of profit to fall is a theory of the mechanism underlying capitalist crises. But the transformation of quantity into quality isn't a mechanism in this sense. It rather generalises the features common to physical and social processes which are produced by a wide variety of different mechanisms. This line of thought suggests that we should see the dialectic of nature as a broad philosophical conception of nature rather than a set of general laws from which more specific ones applicable to particular aspects of the world can be deduced. This way of thinking about the dialectic of nature has the advantage that it rules out the kind of dogmatic dictation to working scientists which gave the idea a bad name under Stalinism, but it implies a fairly loose and open relationship between dialectical philosophy and scientific research which ought to be explicitly recognised.

My second and more substantive reservation concerns John's defence of *History and Class Consciousness* in chapter 5. His aim here is in particular to address criticisms of Lukacs from an Althusserian standpoint, notably in a well known article by Gareth Stedman Jones.[19] Lukacs conceives historical materialism as essentially the self consciousness of the working class. It is because the transformation of labour power into a commodity is the basis of capitalist society that only from workers' standpoint is it possible to develop an objective understanding of that society. Lukacs calls the proletariat the 'absolute subject-object of history': in the process of struggling to defend its interests, the working class is able increasingly both to comprehend and take hold of history. Stedman Jones argues that by equating Marxism with class consciousness Lukacs reduces historical materialism to a theory of class subjectivity, dissolving the objective structures (the forces and relations of production) within which class struggles unfold.

John vigorously rebuts this argument, making many very effective points. It is worth noting, however, that this defence relies on a *recon-struction* of what Lukacs says. *History and Class Consciousness* is a collection of essays composed over a period of several years, some of which were redrafted. They reflect the absorption and reinterpretation of the classical Marxist tradition by someone who was already a mature philosopher with a substantial body of work (notably *The Theory of the Novel*) before he became a Marxist. Lukacs later described his pre-Marxist position as that of 'Romantic anti-capitalism'. Heavily influenced by the sociologists Max Weber and Georg Simmel, he saw the position of humankind as a tragic one, caught up in a fragmented and meaningless modern world from which any sense of understanding things as a whole had been lost. His astonishing rapid conversion to rev-olutionary Marxism in 1918 led Lukacs to see the proletariat as the source of this missing totality. Initially this led him into what Michael Löwy calls a kind of revolutionary 'messianism', in which the proletariat functions as a kind of seventh cavalry.[20] This meant that, in 1918-1921, he often took up quite ultra-left positions within the Communist International.

Gradually, as a result in particular of Lenin's *Left-Wing Communism* (1920) and the debates at the Third Congress of the Comintern (1921), Lukacs moved towards a much more mature understanding of revolu-tionary Marxism. *History and Class Consciousness* records this process. Thus, the great essay 'Reification and the Consciousness of the Proletariat' which dominates the book, is a series of brilliant discussions of both Marx's texts and bourgeois classical philosophy conducted at a high level of theoretical abstraction. While it is clear that he does not, as his critics claim, simply equate Marxist theory with what workers actu-ally think at any given time and that he sees the development of revolutionary consciousness as a process rather than an instanteous act, the essay contains a number of problematic formulations, as do some of the others composed earlier. Thus John himself points out that Lukacs' claim that Marxist orthodoxy consists solely in its method and his equa-tion of this method with the concept of totality carries with it definite idealist dangers.[21]

The last two essays in the book, a defence of the Bolsheviks from Luxemburg's criticisms and 'Towards a Methodological of the Problem of Organisation' reflect the full impact on Lukacs of the debates in 1920-1921. Along with the essay on Lenin written very shortly afterwards, they in some ways offer a corrective to the ambiguities and hostages to fortune that occur elsewhere in the book. What John does in defending Lukacs is to draw on these essays and to highlight relatively brief remarks in the 'Reification' essay in order to provide a rebuttal to the critics; he also brings in Gramsci's discussion of 'contradictory consciousness', which provides a concrete historical framework for understanding the development of class consciousness quite absent in Lukacs. At one level, this is fair enough, but it involves constructing a kind of ideal type of *History and Class Consciousness* which fails to capture the unevennesses in the essays and the process of development they record.

One advantage of highlighting the evolving and incomplete character of Lukacs' essays is that it draws attention to what is at once perhaps the most exciting and most tragic moment in the entire history of classical Marxism. The impact of the First World War and the October Revolution won many gifted intellectuals to revolutionary Marxism—chief among them Lukacs and Gramsci. When they came to the Communist movement they were marked by their intellectual background (in the case of both Lukacs and Gramsci it was one dominated by different forms of idealism) and by the weaknesses of the left in their native countries. Between the end of the First World War and the mid-1920s we see them grappling with the twin problem of renewing a Marxist tradition corrupted by the Second International and building mass revolutionary parties in complex and rapidly changing conditions. As a result of this experience, and of the leadership offered to the Third International by Lenin and Trotsky, we see these very gifted revolutionaries mature as Marxists in the mid-1920s—a process reflected in the later essays of *History and Class Consciousness* and in Lukacs' *Lenin,* and in Gramsci's 1926 'Lyons Theses'. Revolutionary Marxism thus seems on the verge of a quantum leap forward, both politically and intellectually.

And then this process is brutally cut short by history—by the defeat of the German Revolution, the Stalinist degeneration of the Russian Revolution, the victory of fascism in Italy and Germany. Lukacs and Gramsci are both in different ways victims of this series of terrible reversals—Gramsci most directly as a prisoner of Mussolini, Lukacs through his efforts to find a way of surviving within an increasingly Stalinised Communist movement. Neither stops thinking and writing, but the thought of both is scarred by the fact that historical conditions have turned dramatically against revolutionaries. Gramsci's *Prison Notebooks* are full of brilliant insights and analyses, but expressed through concepts whose often ambiguous and metaphorical character has too often allowed their exploitation by reformists and worse. Lukacs' later writings are those of an exceptionally gifted thinker, but they are pervaded by a fatalism that reflects his 'right-Hegelian' reconciliation with a historical reality dominated by Stalinism and fascism. It is left to Trotsky to carry on the classical Marxist tradition in its full vigour, but in extremely unfavourable conditions which confine his influence to the margins of the workers' movement.

Hence the significance of *The Algebra of Revolution.* It recaptures the philosophical thread that runs through classical Marxism, and restates and extends this dialectical thought with great clarity and force. It is a work that seeks to restore the continuity of the revolutionary tradition that was broken by Stalin and Hitler, and to make available some of its most creative ideas to a new generation who can apply and develop in the most favourable conditions to have confronted the Marxist tradition since that fatal turning point in the mid-1920s.

Notes

1 G W F Hegel, *The Phenomenology of Spirit* (Oxford, 1977), s20, p11.
2 G W F Hegel, *The Science of Logic* (2 vols, London, 1966), II, p67.
3 K Marx, *Capital,* vol I (Harmondsworth, 1976), p103.
4 For example, L Colletti, *Marxism and Hegel* (London, 1973), and 'Marxism and the Dialectic', *New Left Review* 93 (1975).
5 J Roemer, '"Rational Choice" Marxism', in id, ed, *Analytical Marxism* (Cambridge, 1986), p191.
6 See, for example, M Rosen, *Hegel's Dialectic and its Criticism* (Cambridge, 1982).
7 J Rees, *The Algebra of Revolution* (New Jersey, 1998), p106.
8 Ibid, p107.
9 Ibid, p103.
10 V I Lenin, Collected Works (50 vols, Moscow, 1972), XXXVIII, p319.
11 J Rees, op cit, p109.
12 Ibid, p110.
13 K Marx, *Grundrisse* (Harmondsworth, 1973), p101.
14 K Marx, *Theories of Surplus Value* (3 vols, Moscow, 1963-72), II, p174. For discussions of the development of Marx's concepts in successive economic manuscripts, see V C Vygodski, *The Story of a Great Discovery* (Tunbridge Wells, 1974), and J Bidet, *Que faire du Capital?* (Paris, 1985).
15 J Rees, op cit, p112.
16 P Pomper (ed), *Trotsky's Notebooks 1933-1935* (New York, 1986), pp88-89.
17 See P McGarr, 'Order Out of Chaos', *International Socialism* 2.48 (1990), and 'Engels and Natural Science', ibid, 2.65 (1994).
18 R Bhaskar, *A Realist Theory of Science* (Hassocks, 1978).
19 G Stedman Jones, 'The Marxism of the Early Lukacs', *New Left Review* 70 (1971).
20 M Löwy, *Georg Lukacs—From Romanticism to Bolshevism* (London, 1979), p165.
21 J Rees, op cit, pp247-248.

It's life Jim, but not as we know it

A review of Steven Rose, **Lifelines** *(Penguin, 1997), £20*

JOHN PARRINGTON

Science is neutral and abuses of science are aberrations in an otherwise healthy system—or such is the view of most mainstream philosophers of science and certainly of most working scientists themselves.[1] Therefore to venture beyond attacking those pseudo-scientists responsible for bringing science's good name into disrepute, and to suggest that such abuses are but a symptom of a wider problem in the philosophy of science, might reasonably be expected to cause a certain amount of friction. A geneticist reviewing Steven Rose's new book *Lifelines* in the prestigious science journal *Nature* illustrates the point. On the one hand, he acknowledges how genetics in Nazi Germany 'served as an argument for mass murder', and in the United States it 'was used to legitimise mass sterilisation, laws against racial mixing and a restrictive immigration policy'.[2] Yet he spends the rest of the review blindly defending the mainstream biological reductionism that was used to justify such atrocities. In the end his worst fear appears to be that Rose may be 'successful in selling his idea to young biologists who might read the book'!

It is not only conservative scientists who are a little perturbed by *Lifelines*.[3] This is because in this book Rose goes much further than in previous work, such as the now classic *Not in our Genes*[4], which largely concentrated on the immediate task of challenging the views of the sociobiologists. The most notorious of these, Richard Dawkins, went so far as to argue that human beings are merely 'robots...blindly programmed to preserve the selfish molecules known as genes'.[5] *Not in our*

Genes was a marvellous polemic that provided crucial ammunition in the battle of ideas that raged in biology during the mid-1980s. In contrast, *Lifelines* has a more ambitious goal. It sets out to challenge the much wider set of assumptions that the reductionist programme is ultimately based upon, and which is still accepted by the majority of biologists. In doing so it also provides an alternative, far more sophisticated 'dialectical' viewpoint.

Still putting out fires

One of the co-authors of *Not in our Genes*, Richard Lewontin, previously commented that fighting biological determinism is like putting out fires.[6] Every time you extinguish one, another starts somewhere else. In fact there has been a rise in biological determinist arguments in the 1990s, partly for ideological reasons, and partly because of the acceleration in genetic technology, the pinnacle of which is the current human genome project.[7] So a part of Rose's argument consists of bringing up to date and expanding some of the concepts developed in previous work. He points out that one of the ways in which complex social behaviour becomes labelled as having a biological basis is by what he describes as 'reification'. This means converting a dynamic process into a static phenomenon. In practice it can result in lumping together all sorts of diverse social activities as if they had one unitary cause.

One example has been the way biological explanations have been put forward to explain 'violence'.[8] One of the bogeys raised by tabloids and politicians in the 1990s has been the idea that there is a rising spiral of 'inner city violence'.[9] How convenient it would be if violence in society was found to be, not a social problem, but due to 'bad genes'. Rose describes how, in the biological determinist's eyes, acts of violence as disparate as 'a man abusing his lover or child, fights between football fans, strikers resisting police, racist attacks on ethnic minorities, and civil and national wars' are all seen as manifestations of 'aggression'.[10] It is of course assumed that this must be the same 'aggression' that is measured as the time taken for a laboratory rat to kill a mouse placed in its cage— so called 'muricidal' behaviour! The search then begins for the genes that cause this phenomenon. The description of what such genetic 'research' actually involves is worth dwelling on here because it shows, on the one hand, the flawed assumptions that guide such work, and on the other, the total lack of scientific rigour that would never survive in any other field of biology.

Rose discusses the case of a Dutch family, some of whose male members were abnormally violent, their behaviour including 'aggressive outbursts, arson, attempted rape and exhibitionism'. All the men possessed a mutation in a gene coding for an enzyme, monoamine oxidase, associated with production of a chemical produced by the brain. Eventually the author of the study dissociated himself from his previous claim that there could be a unitary cause for the widely different behaviour patterns. But this didn't prevent, two years later, a paper appearing in the prestigious journal *Science*, describing a study of mice which had been genetically engineered to lack the enzyme.[11] It was noted that the mice showed 'trembling, difficulty in righting, fearfulness, frantic running and falling over...disturbed sleep...propensity to bite the experimenter...hunched posture'. Yet of all these features the authors only highlighted 'aggression' in the paper's title! When Rose raised this point in a letter to *Science*, he was telephoned by one of the authors who explained they had highlighted aggression in this way because it seemed the best way of drawing attention to their results! Rose points out that this sort of evidence is being used by the US Federal Violence Initiative, which aims to identify inner city children regarded as 'at risk' of becoming violent in later life due to predisposing biochemical or genetic factors.[12]

Reductionist method and reductionist philosophy

Many scientists would accept Rose's criticisms of the studies we have just mentioned. He faces a much larger obstacle in seeking to challenge reductionism as a whole. One of the main problems is the very success of the reductionist method. As Rose points out, the power of modern science lies in the fact that it is about more than just passively observing and recording the natural world. Instead scientists seek to understand the world by 'actively intervening in it, by first controlling it and then experimenting on it'. By necessity this approach must be reductive, because 'it works by attempting to isolate from the flux of the everyday world just the one aspect, the phenomenon that we wish to study, and then changing one at a time the conditions we believe may affect it'.[13] In biology, the words of Alexander Pope may be true: 'Life following life through creatures you dissect, you lose it in the moment you detect',[14] but it is also true that the power of modern medicine and the dizzying pace of molecular biology over the last few decades draw their strength from such a reductive approach.

A problem arises, however, when the power of the reductionist method becomes confused with the idea that the natural world really exists in such an atomised form. Reductionist method becomes reductionist philosophy and thus we get scientists like James Watson, one of the co-discoverers of the helical structure of DNA, arguing that, 'There is only one science, physics; everything else is social work'.[15] As Rose points out, such a view is nonsensical because it misses completely the fact that true understanding of the natural world can only come about through a combination of analysis from different levels. To understand what takes place when a frog jumps after a fly for instance, what Watson would see as the most 'fundamental' level, ie the atomic structure of the molecules in the frog's muscle, would explain little. We also need biochemistry to understand the chemical changes taking place, physiology to comprehend the nerve-muscle connections, ecology to understand the life pattern of the frog and its interactions with other species, and so on.

Rose's point is that although science has created a hierarchy of analysis, we should not be fooled into thinking this reflects a hierarchy in nature itself. What is happening at the different levels is happening simultaneously, not as part of some cause and effect chain. But Rose also makes it clear that if we are to go beyond reductionism, we must also provide a new way of understanding how these different levels fit together. And the only philosophical viewpoint that can really get to grips with the complexity of the interactions taking place is a dialectical one.[16]

It is here that I have a certain criticism of Rose. He is quite correct in his argument about how the philosophy of reductionism stifles a correct understanding of the natural world. But I think he sometimes underestimates the extent to which a dialectical way of looking at things can often be forced upon scientists, even if they do not consciously acknowledge it, precisely because in a number of emerging fields it is impossible to understand the phenomena one is looking at in any other way. This has occurred in two particular areas which Rose himself dwells upon—chaos and complexity theory on the one hand,[17] and my own field of embryology on the other. The first area has already been discussed from a dialectical standpoint in this journal.[18] It is undoubtedly true that a dialectical viewpoint could have greatly aided the transition to a more sophisticated understanding in the field of embryology. However, it is also true that without the empirical discoveries, often achieved with the most reductive methodology, the only point that a dialectical viewpoint could supply would be vague generalisations. Dialectical 'laws' are still best illuminated through nature in all its messy concreteness, however haphazard may have been the path that led us to such knowledge.[19]

The problem of metaphor

If Rose can be criticised for his underestimation of some scientists' ability to transcend their reductionist philosophy under force of circumstance, this is a minor point when viewed against the success of *Lifelines'* critique of reductionist philosophy. The book succeeds not only in its scope, but also in the way it draws together a number of important conceptual advances which have been germinating in Rose's earlier work and in the work of others who seek an alternative to reductionism in science.[20] The rest of this review will look at what I consider to be the most important strands.

We have already seen how Rose challenges the idea that human behaviour is determined by our genes. But he also challenges the very notion of what constitutes a gene. In particular he questions the way in which DNA, the stuff out of which genes are made, has become symbolised as the 'blueprint' of life. One important point that Rose makes is about the role of metaphors in biology. He discusses how changes in the workings of society as a whole are often passed on metaphorically to biology. Thus, 'brains, once perceived as functioning on hydraulic principles, and later as telephone exchanges, are now supercomputers, another part of biology's information highway'.[21] In descriptions of the living cell, we find that,

> ...in the biochemical literature of the 1930s to the 1950s, cells were pictured as small factories, with 'powerhouses' (mitochondria) and energy currency systems (ATP), whose central function was maintaining a balanced energy budget...by the 1980s energy budgets had been relegated to a minor league. Dominant now were concepts of control processes and information flow within the cell, whose functions were no longer seen in terms of crude energy, but of sophisticated management.[22]

It was information technology that supplied the metaphor for DNA almost from the moment of its discovery in 1953 by Crick and Watson—from now on it became viewed as a 'code'.[23] In line with this, it became part of the 'central dogma' of molecular biology that the passage of information from DNA to the proteins it specified was a one way trip.[24] Even the language molecular biologists use to describe this process—*transcription* of DNA into RNA (the intermediary molecule), *translation* of RNA into protein—betray the origins of the metaphor in information theory. Now, in many ways the metaphor has been a very valuable one. The idea of a linear code has become one of the great concepts of biology. The problem is that its very success is in danger of obscuring our true knowledge of DNA's place in the cell.

The problem with the DNA centred view

The main problem with the DNA centred view is that the 'central dogma' is simply not true. As Rose tells us: 'Far from being isolated in the cell nucleus, magisterially issuing orders by which the rest of the cell is commanded...genes are in constant dynamic exchange with their cellular environment'.[25] Rose refers to the idea developed by complexity theorist Stuart Kaufmann of the 'cellular web'.[26] As an analogy, consider a piece of weaving:

> [This] *has a pattern, which resides not in any of the individual threads which constitute the warp and weft of the fabric, but in the product of their interactions. Furthermore, although the threads are individually quite weak, woven together they have considerable strength. And perhaps even more relevant, neither the pattern nor the strength depends on any one 'master thread'. Remove any individual thread and the pattern, strength and stability of the fabric are only marginally affected.*

It is similar with the network of cellular components:

> *Once it reaches a sufficient degree of complexity, it becomes strong, stable and capable of resisting change; the stability no longer resides in the individual components, the enzymes, their substrates and products, but in the web itself. The more interconnections, the greater the stability and the less the dependence on any one individual component.*[27]

We can only really get to grips with the role of DNA in the cell by understanding its place within this cellular network. What this means in practice is that it is not simply the case that the cellular contents are read off from the DNA 'code', because the DNA itself can only be expressed through its interaction with other components of the cell. As Rose argues:

> *In the digital information metaphor, these cellular mechanisms play no part... They are as dumb as the mechanism by which a cassette player converts the trace on a magnetic tape into a Beethoven violin concerto or a Miles Davis jazz track. All that the tape head and the speakers do is to follow the instructions given by the tape. They can influence the quality and the fidelity of the sound that is emitted, but they don't carry information. The symphony remains in the DNA. But this is not how cells work. Unlike the cassette player, they don't merely play their 'tape' at constant speed and hang the consequences. They instruct the tape as to which bits to play and when to play them, and they also edit the output. And of course, also quite unlike the cassette player, they continually reconstruct themselves throughout the cell cycle and the lifetime of the organism which they comprise. In so far as the information metaphor is valid at all, it can be expressed only in the dynamic interaction—the dialectic, therefore—between the DNA and the cellular system in which it is embedded. Cells make their own lifelines.*[28]

Dramatic proof of the reliance of gene expression on the cellular environment was provided by the cloning of the sheep Dolly.[29] Dolly's genetic material all came from the udder cell of an adult sheep. In these cells there is a very restricted pattern of gene expression, just enough to cover the specialised components that such cells need. Yet under the influence of the egg into which the udder cell nucleus was transplanted, the restrictions were lifted and the DNA became capable of specifying a whole new sheep's body. Totipotency, a natural feature in plants,[30] had now been achieved.

New views on the origin of life

The 'decentralisation' of DNA's role within the cell raises important issues about how life arose in the first place. We know that the chemicals that make up living cells would soon be burned up in the earth's oxygenated atmosphere if they weren't contained within the protective enclosure of the cell. A major insight was supplied in the 1930s by the Russian scientist Oparin, whose dialectical way of thinking proved crucial.[31] He argued that, originally, the earth's atmosphere must have been quite different from now. Instead of the present highly oxidising atmosphere, it must have been a reducing mixture of hydrogen, ammonia and methane, together with carbon dioxide, exactly the composition that the Galileo probe is now revealing on the surface of Titan, Jupiter's moon.

The present day atmosphere is very different precisely because it is a by-product of life itself, in particular the photosynthesising work of plants. Following Oparin's work it was shown that the major building blocks of life could be created spontaneously in such conditions.[32] However, major questions still remained. How did the living cell itself arise? And at what point did DNA appear on the scene? For those with a DNA centred view the answer is simple. DNA must have arisen first. But given what we have said about the reliance of DNA on the cellular environment, it seems hard to imagine how this could have been the case. In fact, it seems far more plausible, as Rose argues:

> [that the] *presence of the cell membrane boundary, rather than replication, was the first crucial step in the development of life from non-life, for it is this that enables a critical mass of organic constituents to be assembled, making possible the establishment of an enzyme-catalysed metabolic web of reactions. Only subsequently could accurate replication based on nucleic acids have developed.*[33]

In fact, the creation of such a membrane and the concentration within it of the necessary chemical components is a process that can be mimicked experimentally today. In summary then, when DNA did finally arrive on the scene, it must have radically transformed the form of proto-life, but to do so there had to be the pre-existing cellular environment to receive it.[34]

The developing organism

If gene expression is profoundly affected by the state of the cellular environment, it is also true that is meaningless to talk about the 'action' of genes as if they were separate, isolated entities, an approach which Rose derides as the 'beanbag' view of genetics.[35] In a multicellular organism like a human being, the true effects of gene expression only become apparent at the level of the body as a whole. But at this level, what we view as a particular feature, say the colour of the eyes, is in fact only the end product of a complex chain of events involving many different genes.[36]

· We can best see the true significance of these gene interactions if we turn to embryology. Rose points out that there is a major difference between the assembly of a car and that of a foetus. Living organisms are quite different from cars in that:

> ...from very early on in their development they have to be capable simultaneously of a quasi-independent existence, and of growing further towards maturity. Moreover, the attributes that enable them at any one moment to maintain their existence are not always merely 'miniature' forms of those they will need in adulthood.

This is obviously true for some life forms. 'Frogs' eggs become tadpoles become frogs; butterflies' eggs become caterpillars and chrysalises before butterflies emerge. Each stage requires a radical transformation of body plan, yet during each transformation the functions necessary for life must be preserved.' But it is also true in quite subtle ways for organisms which seem to show linear developmental trajectories without such radical breaks. As Rose concludes, 'life demands of all its forms the ability simultaneously to *be* and to *become*'.[37]

The way this is achieved is that the developing organism is subject to two opposing forces—specificity and plasticity. A vivid illustration of these two forces at work is provided by the developing eye.[38] The eye develops in association with its connection to a brain that is also developing. As both eye and brain grow and mature, the connections between them are broken and reformed many times, yet the overall pattern of the relationship between eye and brain must be maintained if vision is not to be impaired. At the same time the developing eye seems to be resistant to environmental 'noise', yet is still sensitive enough to respond to changes in the environment if they are sustained. How is all this achieved? There appear to be 'many alternative routes that the cell and the organism can adopt during development which can lead to an essentially identical end-point. In the presence of a particular gene and protein, one route is adopted, and in their absence another is taken. Once again, there is no linear path between gene and organism'.[39]

How evolution really works

Rose refutes the idea that it is the (selfish) genes themselves that natural selection acts upon. He argues that while selection ultimately *works* through changes in the genes, this is not where selection *acts*.[40] Instead it is action at a distance; it is action at the level of the organism as a whole, as part of a species and finally as part of an interacting ecosystem.

This has major consequences for the mechanism of evolution. Rose puts forward a view in which evolution is constrained by structural considerations, what he calls the 'laws of form'. Its fundamental consequence is that every trait that is selected also carries with it interlinked traits. Or as Rose puts it, if evolution were a menu, it would be *table d'hote*, not *à la carte*! The interconnectedness we have described has major relevance for the increasing evidence that evolution does not take place gradually, as Darwin supposed. Instead it seems that organisms may retain a particular unchanging form for long periods of time; this stability is, however, punctuated by periods when relatively rapid change takes place. One way of explaining this would be, as Rose puts it, that 'genetic variation can be damped, rendered essentially neutral, until such time as it accumulates sufficiently to tip the next generations of organisms into new stable states'.[41] It is one thing to concentrate on the individual organism but there are also further levels at which natural selection can act.

Much evolutionary theory ignores the fact that mutual interactions between organisms are an important feature of nature. Most people will be familiar with the example of plants which produce flowers which encourage bees or other insects to settle on them. Rose draws our attention to even more intricate relationships. For instance certain types of parasitical wasps which lay their eggs in caterpillars turn out to be attracted to the volatile chemicals in caterpillar faeces but they are also attracted to the plants on which the caterpillars feed. The plants have evolved a mechanism for secreting the chemicals to attract the wasps when they, the plants, are attacked by the caterpillars![42] In other words, there is a complexity which means that the idea of a 'balance of nature' with its implicit message of unchanging stability is profoundly mistaken.

Against the new theology of nature

The main reason the *Origin of Species* so shocked Victorian society when it was published was its challenge to the religious idea of an ordered social world and natural world.[43] As Freud put it, the theory 'destroyed man's supposedly privileged place in creation and proved his descent from the animal kingdom and his ineradicable animal nature'. Rose argues that the ultra-Darwinism of Richard Dawkins and his friends actually ends up restoring the old theological vision. There is a fundamental contradiction in Dawkins' argument. It is summed up by his statement that 'we are built as gene machines...but we have the power to turn against our creators. We, alone on earth, can rebel against the tyranny of the selfish replicators'.[44] As Rose points out:

[There is] *something profoundly unsatisfactory about this argument. Either we, like all other living forms, are the product of our genes, or we are not. If we are, it must be that our genes are not merely selfish but rebellious... If, on the other hand, it is not our genes that are rebellious, what other options are available? Dawkins never says but implicit in his argument is that there is some non-material, non-genetic force moulding our behaviour... Thus despite Dawkins' passionately explicit claims to atheism and expressed hostility to religion, the charge against him is that they fail to carry their own genetic argument to its logical conclusion.*[45]

The importance of being human

If this review has largely been full of glowing praise for *Lifelines*, there is one criticism with which it seems apt to end. It hinges upon the use Rose makes of Marx's famous quote that 'men make history, but not in conditions of their own choosing'. He extends the idea to all living organisms. As we have seen, this is of immense value in arguing against the ultra-Darwinist view that living creatures are simply prisoners of their genes, blindly following the DNA 'code'. But there is a danger in stretching the similarity too far. I can agree with most of the following passage from *Lifelines* but not with the last few lines:

Organisms do not sit waiting patiently for nature or the 'environment' to scrutinise them, but rather are actively engaged in working to choose and transform their environments, to adjust and appropriate them to their own ends. Autopoiesis, organisms as active players, is as apparent as when a single-celled organism swims away from a depleted food source towards a rich one as it is when a growing troop of axons from the retina of a cat seek, find and modify their target neurons in the lateral geniculate, in the symbiotic relationship of a leguminous plant with the nodules of nitrogen fixing bacteria in its roots, and in the decision of an impoverished Mexican to cross the border into California or an unemployed Newcastle builder to move to Düsseldorf.[46]

The fact is that the human choices employed here are not the same as the 'choices' that take place in the natural world. Both involve 'active players', but human beings are more than that. The crucial difference is that we also have the capacity to reason and to reflect on our actions, but also to discuss them with other human beings. However constrained were the actions of the Mexican peasant or the Newcastle builder, they were undoubtedly the result of much heart searching and discussions with friends, lovers and family. The other crucial difference in humans 'making history' is that ultimately we have the ability to transcend our current circumstances. And, criticisms aside, as part of that struggle, once again Steven Rose has supplied us with valuable ammunition.

Notes

1   For a fuller, recent discussion of these issues see J Baxter, 'The Return of Political Science' in *International Socialism* 77, pp111-125.
2   B Muller-Hill, 'Life's Dead Letter', *Nature* 390 (1997), p36. Note the contrast with another review, published in the *New Scientist*, which, some quite valid criticisms aside, could hardly have been more complementary. Interestingly this was written not by a biologist but by a social anthropologist. See T Ingold, 'A Call to Arms', *New Scientist* 22, November 1997.
3   At the launch of the new book I heard an interesting comment from a scientist who would probably be considered to be a scientific liberal, Professor Tim Bliss, who made his name in the same field of research into memory as Rose himself. Tim, who is a long standing friend and colleague of Rose, and who also happens to be my ex-head of department, confided to me that he thought this time Steven 'had gone a little too far'. The present state of research into memory, and both Bliss and Rose's place within it, is described in Rose's previous book, *The Making of Memory* (Bantam, 1992).
4   S Rose, R C Lewontin, and L Kamin, *Not in our Genes* (Penguin, 1984).
5   R Dawkins, *The Selfish Gene* (Oxford University Press, 1976).
6   Lewontin serves as a volunteer firefighter in Vermont. He of course himself has a distinguished service record in the battle against biological determinism, with books like *The Dialectical Biologist* (co-written with Richard Levins), (Harvard University Press, 1985); and *The Doctrine of DNA* (Penguin, 1991).
7   For more on the human genome project see J Baxter 'More than its Parts', in L German and R Hoveman (eds), *A Socialist Review* (Bookmarks, 1998), ch 59.
8   For an example see W W Gibbs, 'Seeking the Criminal Element', in *Scientific American*, March 1995, pp76-83.
9   In fact in Britain a new survey has shown that the picture peddled by politicians and the media of an ever rising tide of violent crime is a myth. See *Socialist Worker*, 10 January 1998, p2.
10   S Rose, *Lifelines* (Penguin, 1997), p280.
11   Ibid, p281-282. For further criticism of these studies, see 'Not by our Genes Alone', Editorial in *New Scientist*, 25 February 1995, p3.

12   S Rose, *Lifelines*, op cit, p282. My own experience of the way this 'research' is taken increasingly seriously was attending the 1994 International Biophysics Conference in San Francisco and finding a whole session on this area.

13   Ibid, pp27-28. As Rose reminds us, the reductionist method was first put forward as a scientific strategy by Francis Bacon, who was so dedicated to furthering scientific knowledge that he died in the pursuit of it. While travelling through Highgate in London, he got out of his coach in the middle of winter to see if snow would preserve meat. He caught a chill and passed away soon after!

14   Quoted in S Rose, *Lifelines*, op cit, p21.

15   Quoted ibid, p8.

16   In this, Rose is of course following on from a long tradition in Marxism, from Engels' *Dialectics of Nature* (Moscow, 1972) to Levins and Lewontins' *The Dialectical Biologist* (Harvard University Press, 1985). For a further discussion of the use of dialectical theory in science, see P McGarr, 'Engels and Natural Science', in *International Socialism* 65, pp143-200.

17   Ibid.

18   The two scientists most associated with discovery of the so called homeotic genes, Ed Lewis and Christiane Nusslein-Vollhard, subsequently received the Nobel Prize.

19   As the great Marxist psychologist Lev Vygotsky pointed out, a dialectical science 'has to be built [by discovering] the essence of the given area of phenomena, the laws according to which they change'. In other words, there are no short cuts—L S Vygotsky, *Mind in Society* (Harvard University Press, 1978) p8. I myself remember writing an essay during the final year of my degree, shortly after I had read *Not in our Genes*, criticising the model of body polarity as it then stood, and suggesting a different one based on interactions between the genes. The reality turned out to be far more complex and dialectical than I could have imagined then!

20   Rose draws on the work of Lewontin, Levins, Gould and Stuart Kaufmann in particular, but what is interesting too is how much continuity there has been with earlier radical scientific thinkers in the 1930s. In particular, both the Communist Party influenced scientific left in the 1930s and Soviet thinkers turn out to have influenced a much wider layer of more liberal scientists than I had suspected. So, for instance, genetics in the young Soviet Union adopted a very sophisticated stance and, despite being effectively destroyed by Stalin and his protege Trofim Lysenko, its influence survived into the US genetic tradition, via Theodosius Dobzhansky, who left Russia for the United States at the end of the 1920s and who later influenced Lewontin! See S Rose *Lifelines*, op cit, pp216-217.

21   Ibid, p53.

22   Ibid, p52.

23   It was probably no coincidence that Crick was formerly a physicist who worked on radar in the war and thus was familiar with the new science of cybernetics. For what is still probably the best account of the discovery of DNA, see H Judson, *The Eighth Day of Creation* (Cape, 1979).

24   As Crick put it, 'Once information has passed into the protein it cannot get out again.' Quoted in S Rose, *Lifelines*, op cit, p120.

25   S Rose, *Lifelines*, op cit, p125.

26   See S Kaufmann, *At Home in the Universe: the Search for the Laws of Complexity* (Viking, 1995), which is a brilliant development of complexity theory.

27   S Rose, *Lifelines*, op cit, p164.

28   Ibid, p130.

29   For the background to Dolly, see J Parrington and P Morgan, 'Seeing Double' in *Socialist Review* 207, pp18-19. For the latest developments see *New Scientist*, 17 January 1998.

30   Totipotency in plants is often demonstrated in school classrooms by taking a sliver of carrot and placing it in water, after which it will grow into a complete new plant.

31   A Oparin, *The Origin of Life on Earth* (Macmillan, 1938). See also J B S Haldane's seminal article 'The Origin of Life' in *On Being the Right Size and Other Essays* (Oxford University Press, 1985).

32   This was the work of Stanley Miller in the US, who synthesised amino acids, the building blocks of proteins, in simulated primitive earth conditions.

33   S Rose, *Lifelines*, op cit, p254.

34   As Rose mentions, it is increasingly thought that the intermediary molecule between DNA and proteins, RNA, may have appeared first. See ibid, pp269-270.

35   Ibid, p216.

36   Ibid, p115.

37   Ibid, p142.

38   Ibid, pp142-143.

39   Ibid, pp132-133.

40   Of course the transmission belt of selection is that certain gene mutations become favoured over others, but the act of selection is indirect and mediated through the higher levels described by Rose.

41   S Rose, *Lifelines*, op cit, pp235-236.

42   Ibid, pp227-228.

43   For the background to the reaction to evolutionary theory see A Desmond and J Moore, *Darwin* (Michael Joseph, 1991).

44   R Dawkins, op cit, p215.

45   S Rose, *Lifelines*, op cit, p214.

46   Ibid, p245.

Robin Hood: earl, outlaw or rebel?

*A review of J C Holt, **Robin Hood** (Thames and Hudson, 1991) £ 6.95;
S Knight, **Robin Hood: a complete study of the English outlaw**
(Blackwell, 1994) £16.99; J Ritson, **Robin Hood** (Routledge, 1997) £125*

JUDY COX

Robin Hood is easily the most enduringly popular of all the legendary
heroes of the past. He makes his first appearance in literature as far back
as 1377 in a poem called *Piers Plowman*, where the character called
Sloth says:

> *I do not know my paternoster perfectly as the priest sings it.*
> *But I know rhymes of Robin Hood and Randolph, earl of Chester*
>
> *(I Kan noght parfitly my Paternoster as the Priest it syngeth,*
> *But I kan rymes of Robyn hood and Randolf Erl of Chestre.)*[1]

Medieval minstrels sang tales of Robin Hood across the length and
breadth of Britain. In Tudor England Robin led the tremendously popular
May Games and the oral tradition of ballads about him remained very
popular. He pops up in Shakespeare's plays, and his was the name adopted
by radical candidates in elections which preceded the English Revolution.
Robin was a character in Walter Scott's *Ivanhoe* and he also scaled the literary heights, making appearances in poems by Keats and Tennyson.

In the 20th century he has been played by the most charismatic of
screen idols, Douglas Fairbanks Senior and Errol Flynn and, more
recently, by the somewhat less charismatic Kevin Costner. Robin has
made an effortless transition to television, with several programmes such
as the popular 1980s series, *Robin of Sherwood*, and the ongoing feminist

children's programme, *Maid Marion and her Merry Men*.

Few of the other heroes of the past have survived to be household names into the 21st century. Who today tells tales of Hereward the Wake, scourge of the Norman invaders, or Eustace the Monk, soldier of fortune, or Fulk fitz Warin, a Welsh warrior who took up arms against King John?[2] In comparison with Robin, even King Arthur has faded into the mists of time. What, then, is the secret of Robin's phenomenal success? Was he a nobleman reforming the worst excesses of the system, then becoming reconciled with the King and the established order, a truly British hero? Is he the representative of a supra-historical yearning for an idyllic rural past, where the sun always shone, as the heritage industry would have us believe? Or is he a symbol of resistance to tyranny, whose legend has endured because in every age people have sought ways to oppose the oppression they faced?[3]

Noble outlaw or outlawed noble?

For many people the archetypal Robin Hood is the character played by Erroll Flynn in the 1938 film. He is a wronged nobleman who challenges the tyranny of bad King John and is restored to his rightful position, his lands and his lover by good King Richard, who returns from the crusades in the nick of time. However, this widely accepted tale of Robin has little in common with the Robin Hood legend in its earlier years. One of the earliest elements of the legend is a series of ballads, probably written between 1400 and 1500, which established many lasting features of the Robin Hood story, such as wicked sheriffs, gallows rescues, cunning disguises and archery contests. Today these are familiar as the stuff of children's cartoons, but these ballads were written from the perspective of poor farmers and artisans.[4] The simple, often extremely violent stories give a sense of opposition between the natural social order of the outlaws in the forest and the new relationships associated with the developing towns, with their legal restrictions, acquisitiveness and prisons.

In one of the earliest ballads, *Robin Hood and the Monk*, there is a sense that the solidarity of the outlaws and the freedom of the forests provide security against the alien, corrupting forces of organised religion and the legal system. Another early ballad, *Robin and the Potter*, reveals the monetary edge to the restrictions of the town, which one historian has interpreted as expressing artisans' dislike of producing artefacts for the market, 'an early vision of alienated labour'.[5] Historian Stephen Knight provides an insight into the early popularity of the Robin Hood ballads: 'The semi-mythical sense of resistance and opposition to the 'statutory' forces of state, church and emergent mercantilism seems deeply embedded in these tales and references, and they are a major mode of opposing those forces in the cultural consciousness of the late medieval period'.[6] Seen in this context, many familiar themes of the Robin Hood stories gain a new dimension. For example, the theme of disguise, often as a state or church official, has a sense of undermining authority that has radical potential, as does the theme of liberating those imprisoned and condemned by the state, or the rescue of women forced into marriages against their will.

It seems likely that the ballads were sung to audiences of common people, yeomen and artisans. For example, in the later ballads there are several 'Robin Meets his Match' storylines. Various artisans, such as potters, butchers, and tanners, all give Robin a thrashing before being accepted by the outlaws. Historians Dobson and Taylor have associated the proliferation of fighting artisans with the growth in importance and self consciousness of tradesmen in this period, as if each trade sooner or later fits itself into a Robin Hood ballad, or a crowd pleasing minstrel does it for them.

The most famous of all the early ballads, *A Lytell Gest of Robin Hood*, was so popular it was reprinted seven times by the mid-15th century. In the *Gest* there are many traditional features and characters of the legend, but Robin does not give what he acquires to the poor, in fact the only charity he shows is to a poor knight. Many historians have used this to dismiss the radical edge of the early legend.[7] However, it can also be argued that the *Gest* echoes the values of a feudal world where actual money meant little because, in feudal terms, 'use value rather than cash nexus', taking people in, giving them protection, food, clothing, would have been seen as more beneficial than a cash prize.[8] Another historian has compared the *Gest*'s sympathy for the knight with the ideas expressed in the Peasants' Revolt of 1381, where rebels retained their allegiance to the crown and to the idea of a true religion, however violent their hatred for the king's courtiers, churchmen and other agents of what they felt to be an unfairly oppressive state.[9] On this basis the relatively sympathetic portrayal of the knight is compatible with a rebellious attitude towards the ruling order in general.

In addition, the *Gest* provides evidence that opposition to oppression was central to the early legend. At the beginning of the *Gest*, Little John asks Robin for instructions and Robin replies that he must be good to the poor and to knights and squires that 'will be good fellows' but bishops and archbishops must be beaten on sight and the sheriff is the ultimate target:

> *But see you do no farmer harm,*
> *that tills with his plough.*
> *Neither the good yeoman*
> *that walks by the greenwood shade:*
> *Nor no knight or Squire*
> *that will be a good fellow.*

But these bishops and these archbishops,
You shall beat and bind,
And the high sherriff of Nottingham
Keep him on your mind.

(But loke ye do no Husbonde harme,
that tilleth with his ploughe.
No more ye shall no gode yeoman
That walketh by the grene-wode shawe:
Ne no knyght, ne no squyer
That wol be a gode felawe.

But, thesse Bishoppes and these Archbishoppes
You shall them bete and bynd
The Hye sherif of Notyingham
Hym holde ye in your mynde.)

As Knight points out, 'The *Gest*, after all, advocates massive theft
from the church, civic insurrection against and murder of a properly
appointed Sheriff, breach of legitimate agreement with a King.' It is 'a
story with much potency among people who experience institutionalised
oppression and therefore require the relief of fictional forms of dissent'.[10]
The Robin Hood ballads were a major focus for the idea that oppressive
authorities can be resisted, even if this usually remained an aspiration
rather than an active opposition.

The tradition of the ballads was, therefore, a very powerful one. 'For
centuries Robin Hood was a symbol of independence, of resistance to
authority in church or state. This concept is central to the whole saga and
particularly prominent in the early ballads'.[11] However, the association of
Robin Hood with the aspirations of the oppressed was not limited to the
ballads. In the 1440s Walter Bower wrote *Scotichronicon*, a history of
Scotland and England. The book contains this passage about the year
1296: 'Then arose the famous murderer, Robert Hood, as well as Little
John, together with their accomplices from among the dispossessed,
whom the foolish populace are so inordinately fond of celebrating both
in tragedy and comedy'.[12] Two centuries later in 1640 during elections in
Somerset for what turned out to be the Short Parliament, an opposition
group known as 'Robins' and 'Little Johns' stood a candidate to whom
they referred as Robin Hood.[13]

By the 16th century the idea of poor, rural, freedom as opposed to
urban, propertied, restrictions was well established. This was a strong
theme in the 16th century Robin Hood ballads, and in 17th century plays
such as Richard Brome's *A Jovial Crew*, written in 1641. As the enforced
enclosures of the common land and the superceding of old protective

customs by new laws grew in pace, the newly destitute joined the droves of beggars and vagabonds who had always populated the countryside. It was possible for a bonded peasant or wage labourer to look with envy on those who dispensed with all social ties and responsibilities and lived in liberty in the forests.

As well as embodying this image of rural liberty, Robin Hood, Friar Tuck and Maid Matilda or Marian, were central characters in the May Games which were a very popular rural custom, traditionally encouraged by the wealthy landowners. They were festivals in which people dressed up, drank and danced and demanded money for the church or charity. For example, in 1607 churchwardens in St Cuthbert's parish, needed money to repair a bell so they held a 'church ale' with a procession involving not only Robin Hood, but also Noah and his ark, St George and his dragon, the Sultan of Egypt, morris dancers and giants.[23] Historian David Underdown has described how in the mid-15th century the May Games were part of a very rich tradition of religious plays, civic processions and pageantry: 'In Cornwall and other counties miracle plays still flourished, and even the small Somerset village of Croscombe could promote an annual cycle of plays and revels, complete with Robin Hood and folk heroes'.[24]

However, the May Games also embodied a potential undermining of traditional authority and created the conditions for unlicensed sexual behaviour. A Scottish historian, John Major, wrote in 1551 that the May celebrations were 'kept in a tavern, not a church, in such intemperance of eating and drinking as is the enemy of chastity, in dances and lewd songs that are equally her foe'.[25] In 1549 Bishop Hugh Latimer referred to a visit he made to a town where the church stood empty on a Sunday because, he was told, 'it is Robin Hoode's day. The parishe are gone abroad to gather for Robyn Hoode'.[26]

The establishment was increasingly concerned by the general freedom for the sexes to mingle, drink and dance together provided by the May Games. By the early 17th century Puritan writers and preachers thundered with increasing ferocity against what remained of the 'heathenish' and popish revellings.[27] However, as David Underdown has noted, 'the concern for order was not unique to Puritans, but was a product of the widening gulf between the substantial people 'of credit and reputation' and the disorderly poor'.[28] The growing, centralising state of the period became increasingly hostile to the Games. Christopher Hill explains why: 'The games also offered open defiance to authority, an alternative to the rule of gentry, freemen of boroughs and the hierachy of the church.' The symbolic radicalism in the May rituals, the character of Robin Hood and the enforced collection of money, could easily spill over into more overt gestures of rebellion. In 1439 Sir Piers Venables of

Tutbury and his gang rescued a friend from the Sheriff:

In manner of war, riot, route and insurrection arrayed with force and arms and made a rescue, and took away the said John Forman with them...in manner of insurrection, went into the woods in that country, as if they were Robin Hood and his men; and now they come at different times to Scropton.

(In manere of werre, riote, route and insurrection arriaed with force and armes and made a rescours, and toke awey the saide John Forman for theyme ...in manere of insurrection, wente into the wodes in that contre, like as it hadde be Robyn hode and meyne; and so after that tyme they come diverse tymes withinne the fraunchise atte Scropton forsaide.)[29]

At Southacre, in Norfolk, in 1441, a group of over enthusiastic revellers blocked the road singing, 'We arn Robynhodesmen, war war war,' and threatening to murder a certain Sir Geoffrey Harsyk. In 1498 there were the beginnings of a Robin Hood riot, when a group gathered to rescue two men arrested for assault. Roger Marshall of Westbury, Staffordshire, defended himself in the Star Chamber on the charge of leading riotous assembly to Willenhall under the name of Robin Hood.[30]

Given these events it is not suprising that in 1555 the Scottish parliament banned any annual celebrations involving Robin, Little John, the Abbot of Unreason or the Queen of the May. Anyone involved in choosing such characters could face five years imprisonment, and anyone chosen to play the parts faced exile. However, banning the Games did not put an end to them. John Knox in his 1561 history wrote that in Edinburgh apprentices and craftsmen gathered 'efter the auld wikket manner of Robyn Hoode' and then 'the rascal Multitude were stirred-up to make a Robin-Hood, which enormity was of many years left off and condemned by Statute and Act of Parliament; yet would they not be forbidden, but would disobey and trouble the Town'.[31]

This tradition of festivals, with which Robin was so identified, died out in the century following the Restoration, with the expansion of towns, the growth of the urban middle classes and more strictly polarised rural communities. This was not however, before poor Robin was enlisted by the ruling class to the service of the crown, which was desperately trying to re-establish its authority after the Restoration:

Robin Hood, for centuries a symbol of popular independence and resistance to authority, was quickly pressed into service. As part of the Cornonation celebration at Nottingham in 1661 a short play was enacted in which Robin's traditional loyalty to King Richard was carefully exaggerated...[32]

However, even before the Restoration, Robin had begun a process of gentrification. Firstly Robin 'being of base stock was advanced to the noble dignity of an Earl' and then he later acquired an inherited peerage.[14] Representative of this process were two influential plays by Andrew Munday, the *Downfall of* and *Death of Robert, Earl of Huntingdon*, written in 1598. One possible reason for Munday's granting Robin nobility may have been that the success of his play depended on the patronage of the court who liked to see themselves cast in heroic mode. Christopher Hill suggests that the impact of Munday's play was such that 'from the early 17th century the "tales of Robin Hood" came to be regarded as plebeian, perhaps in reaction to the attempt of Munday and others to make him a peer'.[15] The political significance of the character of Robin Hood must have certainly come into sharper focus in the 1590s, years of famine and social unease which laid the basis for Shakespeare's most political play, *Coriolanus*.

However, the attempt to upgrade Robin socially was concerted and sustained and probably reflected more long term social changes. In the early 16th century the crown tightened the royal forest laws which brought the king into conflict not only with servants, paupers and beggars but with the aristocracy and the gentry. As the crown attempted to impose its claim to ownership of the forests and the animals living in them it came into conflict with traditional ways of living both among the poor and the landed gentry. The gentrification of Robin could have reflected the fact that sections of the propertied classes were in conflict with the crown. There was 'open warfare over hunting rights, often in gangs led by gentlemen against peers or the crown. Aristocratic and gentry feuds were an inescapable part of the social and political scene in Tudor and early Stuart England...'[16]

Whatever the direct cause, many Robin Hood stories of the time show the process of gentrification, and their authors appear anxious not to enhance the status of secular heroes from among the common people. Martin Parker's *A True Tale of Robin Hood*, 1632, describes itself as 'A briefe touch of the life and death of that Renowned outlaw, Robert, Earl of Huntingdon, vulgarly called Robbin Hood who lived and died in 1198'. Some went to great pains to 'prove' Robin's noble birth. In 1795 Dr William Stukeley, Lincolnshire antiquary and fellow of both the Royal Society and the Society of Antiquaries, provided the fictitious earl with a spurious pedigree of Norman nobles, descended from Robert Fitz Ooth who died in 1274, a fiction which was repeated by many and became an accepted part of the tale of Robin Hood.

However, even as the ennoblement of Robin was in full swing, it proved to be impossible to completely separate him from his popular origins. In fact, though his image was cleaned up a bit, he did become a purely aristocratic hero. In fact, he evolved into the archetypal 'social bandit', as Eric Hobsbawm has described it, a noble robber hated by tyrants and authority, but loved and protected by the people.[17] Thus despite Robin's social elevation, Martin Parker acknowledges that he remained a scourge of the rich:

> *But were he knew a miser rich*
> *The poor did oppresse*
> *To feel his coyne his hand did itch*
> *He'd have it more or less.*

While Dr Stukeley was inventing his noble hero, new generations of radical writers were discovering that the story of Robin Hood could provide a means of expressing political opposition to the established order. Joseph Ritson's famous life of Robin Hood was written in 1795, against the backdrop of political and industrial revolution. Initially it was published as two volumes, then as one volume in 1824 which was reprinted throughout the 19th century. The 1824 version of Ritson's *Robin Hood* has recently been reprinted in two beautiful volumes, which includes *A Lytell Gest of Robin Hood*, Martin Parker's *Life of Robin Hood*, and the early ballads discussed above. Unfortunately, the price puts the book outside most people's reach, which is a great shame as the book is fascinating itself and played an important part in the development of the legend. Although Ritson was not the first collector of the Robin Hood stories, his contribution was unique in two ways:

> *He was the first collector to be a convinced radical, an enthusiast for the French Revolution and for Tom Paine's insistence on the Rights of Man; and secondly he was the first major collector to work in a period when, for reasons of rapid social change, many of those who reflected on events and values were interested in looking back to contrast the turbulent present against what had gone before, whether it was imaginary, real or a mixture of the two. At such a time, when overt political dissent was highly dangerous, a story from the past like that of Robin Hood was a suitable medium to convey feelings of a more or less critical character.[18]*

Ironically, given his radical views, Ritson followed earlier work in asserting that Robin was the noble Robert Fitz Ooth, Earl of Huntingdon, born 1160. However, Ritson had no doubt as to the radical potential of the story. Ritson's Robin was:

> *a man, who, in a barbarous age, and under a complicated tyranny, displayed a spirit of freedom and independence which has endeared him to the common*

people, whose cause he maintained (for all opposition to tyranny is the cause of the people), and, in spite of the malicious endeavours of pitiful monks, by whom history was consecrated to the crimes and follies of titled ruffians and sainted idiots, to suppress all record of his patriotic exertions and virtuous acts, will render his name immortal.[19]

Ritson showed his republican stance by demanding, 'What better title King Richard could pretend to the territory and people of England than Robin Hood had to the dominion of Barnsdale or Sherwood is a question humbly submitted to the consideration of the political philosopher'.[20]

During the 19th century, as the question of building and reinforcing nationalism become important for the British ruling class, Robin Hood was enlisted in this cause, which was doubly ironic considering his histories as a common thief or a wronged Norman lord. Walter Scott involved Robin, albeit on the sidelines, in his nationalist novel, *Ivanhoe*. In the political polarisation which followed the French Revolution, Scott drew ideological support from an arch-opponent of the French Revolution, Edmund Burke, to create his story of sturdy Saxons opposing the tyranny of their Norman conquerers. It was, however, writers from the other side of the political divide who found themselves turning to Robin Hood in greater numbers.

In fact, in the turbulent years of the early 19th century, the Robin Hood legend increased its fascination for radical writers. In 1817, encouraged by a reprint of Ritson's book and politically stirred up by several high profile sedition cases against radicals, the 'war of the intellectuals' took place when John Keats, Leigh Hunt, Thomas Love Peacock, Walter Scott and Robert Southey all started work on versions of Robin Hood's story. Keats's poem, *To JHR in Answer to his Robin Hood Sonnets*, was probably the most successful of these efforts. It expressed Keats's revulsion at industrialisation and the impact of the cash nexus on direct sensual relations between humans and their natural productivity, as can be seen from this extract:

And if Robin should be cast
Sudden from his turfed grave
And if Marian should have
Once again her forest days,
She would weep and he would craze.
He would swear, for all his oaks
fallen beneath the dockyard strokes,
Have rotted on the briny seas.
She would weep that her wild bees
Sang not to her—strange that honey
Can't be got without hard money.

Thus, in the 19th century, while writers such as Scott were recasting Robin as a symbol of British nationalism, others were refashioning him in his more traditional role as an opponent of the establishment. Another example of this was Thomas Love Peacock's *Maid Marion*, written in 1822. *Maid Marion* satirised the 'growing use of medieval material as a conservative manoeuvre, nostalgia for feudalism and mystique of monarchy'.[21] Tales of Robin Hood certainly retained their popularity with the mass of ordinary people. In 1840 Pierce Egan the Younger, author of a play called *Wat Tyler*, wrote *Robin Hood and Little John: or, the Merry Men of Sherwood Forest*, which was produced in 41 instalments of a 'penny dreadful', and sold 'hundreds of thousands' of copies, a modern echo of the phenomenal success of the medieval ballads.

It was towards the end of the 19th century that the heritage industry began to develop: the Tate Gallery was opened in 1897, the National Trust established in 1895. Heritage was 'anti-urban, anti-modern and in some sense anti-democratic'. It 'replaced religion for many as a value'.[22] The ever popular Robin was a perfect candidate to become a symbol of an idyllic British past. Even today Nottinghamshire County Council promotes Robin Hood, along with what remains of Sherwood Forest, as very marketable symbols of our harmonious past.

There is, after all, a centuries old tradition of Robin Hood in his forest haven, garlanded with flowers, dressed in green, as Shakespeare described the forest of Arden in *As You Like It*: 'there they live like the old Robin Hood of England; they say many young gentlemen flock to him every day and fleet the time carelessly, as they did in the golden world.' However, the real tradition was never a simple celebration of rural life. The legend was so enduring precisely because it evolved to express the popular responses to successive social changes. Eric Hobsbawm argues that the archetypal social bandit of which Robin is the most famous, is a phenomenon which 'seems to occur in all types of human society which lie between the evolutionary phase of tribal and kinship organisation, and modern capitalist and industrial society', and is especially widespread during the transition to agrarian capitalism.[33] The Robin Hood legend was rooted in the widespread desire for liberty amongst the poor, a desire which was rooted in the oppressions of medieval life, and intensified by the social changes of the 16th and 17th century, the brutal enclosures of the land, civil war and encroachment of the market. Another aspect of the social banditry legend was the idea of the primative redistribution of wealth, robbing the rich and giving to the poor, which was central to Robin's legend in all its different guises.

'Many talk of Robin Hood who never shot his bow'

Most research into the legend of Robin Hood has focused on finding the 'real' Robin. In this respect the work of the academics differs little from the work of amateur local historians across Britain. Sadly, as techniques have developed, so successive theories as to the identity of the 'real' Robin have been discredited. One of the first historians to suffer this fate was Joseph Hunter, who published an account of the life of Robin Hood in 1852. He had apparently found evidence which fitted with the narrative of the *Lytell Gest*. In the *Gest* Robin is an outlaw in Barnsdale, near Doncaster, who is reconciled with 'comely King Edward' when the King visits Yorkshire. In the *Gest* Robin joins the King's service, then becomes bored and returns to the forest. Hunter found that a Robert Hood lived in Wakefield up to 1317, and that he disappeared from all records as he would if he were outlawed (or, more typically, dead). Edward II did travel to Yorkshire in 1323 and a Robyn Hode was in his service in March 1324, then left in November of the same year. Sadly, ultraviolet light has revealed that this Robyn Hode was in the king's service in July 1323, before the king went north, and so the case was already disproved before more research revealed that the Robin Hood legend was in full swing well before these dates.[34]

The first recorded criminal named after the legend of Robin Hood, appears in the King's Remembrancer's Memoranda Roll for Berkshire in 1262, which shows that the prior of Sandleford seized the goods of William Robehod, fugitive. By the slimmest chance this record can be matched with the Roll of the Justices for same area. This shows that William, son of Robert Le Fevre, is indicted with two other men and two women for forming a criminal gang of armed robbers. What these records show is that someone changed William's name to 'Robehod' because he was an outlaw. This indicates that the legend of Robin Hood was already going strong in 1262.[35]

This means that the most likely candidates for a 'real' Robin must have lived before that date. One possibility was discovered by L V D Owen in 1936. Owen's candidate makes his first appearance at assizes in York at Michaelmas in 1226. Here, records show that income included 32s.6d for the chattels of Robert Hod, fugitive. The following year when the name appears again it is written in a more colloquial form, as Hobbehod.[36] However, this is not the first recorded Robin Hood who is an outlaw. Between 1213 and 1216 a Robert Hood, servant of the Abbott of Cirencester, killed Ralph of Cirencester in Cirencester. All this suggests that any attempts to identify the 'real' Robin are very rash as new, earlier candidates will almost inevitably be revealed by new research.

If locating the 'real' Robin is a hopeless task, then claiming him for one locality is equally difficult. The history of searching for Robin has revealed that the legend was spread right around Britain throughout the

13th and 14th centuries (by 1438 a ship called Robin Hood was registered as far away as Aberdeen):

> *A pattern begins to emerge of a figure whose functions are found right through Britain, with local occurrences of no clearly rationalised distribution, and no more than a slight concentration in the North Midlands... Whereas the early ballads appear to link with the small towns developing through craft and mercantilism of central and northern England, the plays are recorded as far away as Exeter and Falkirk, all by 1500.*[37]

Given the obvious state of communications in medieval England, this speedy development of the legend points to an amazing popularity from the very beginning. While we cannot know the exact circumstances behind this, we can hazard a guess based on what we do know of early medieval England. Firstly, this was a society racked from top to bottom by violence and repression, a society in which the majority of people were not free and spent their lives toiling on the land. The peasants lived next to royal forests literally teaming with food, where the penalty for poaching was torture and death. This was an era of frequent rebellions, of outlaws fighting wars with the King's armies, an era where becoming an outlaw or choosing the life of a beggar was the only chance of freedom.

Under these conditions, it becomes easier to see the appeal of a hero who not only escapes to freedom and a life of ease, but also returns to protect the weak and take revenge on tyrants. This is why Robin Hood and all the social bandits who succeeded him were so popular. He was a 'righter of wrongs, the bringer of justice and social equity', a robber who steals from the rich to give to the poor, kills only in self defence or justified revenge and can only be defeated by betrayal:

> *Social banditry of this kind in one of the most universal social phenomena known to history, and one of the most amazingly uniform...this uniformity is not the consequence of cultural diffusion, but the reflection of similar situations within peasant societies, whether in China, Peru, Sicily, the Ukraine or Indonesia. Geographically it is found throughout the Americas, Europe, the Islamic world, South and East Asia and even Australia... Otherwise social banditry is universally found, wherever societies are based on agriculture, and consist largely of peasants and landless labourers, ruled, oppressed and exploited by someone else—lords, towns, governments, lawyers or even banks.*[38]

This is the real heart of the Robin Hood legend. Wherever people are oppressed and beaten down by tyrants, but without the means to fight back on their own behalf, they will dream of an avenging hero, one of the people, but with the freedom, courage, and ability to right their wrongs on their behalf. Robin's story has endured because he represents an unquenchable desire for a better society, a desire which down the centuries has adapted in form but not in content: the violent yeoman standing up against the bishops in the ballads; the unruly Robin of the May Games with his challenges to the authority of the church and state; Ritson's radical Robin; Keats's poignant symbol of hostility to capitalist society; Errol Flynn's anti-Nazi Robin[39] and the1950s TV series starring sturdy Richard Greene, and written by Ring Lardner Jr and Ian McLellan, who were blacklisted in McCarthyite witchhunts.

Whether myth or legend, Robin is the embodiment of the aspirations of thousands throughout the centuries. He was a symbol of freedom when the majority lived in serfdom, an enforcer of natural justice when most were powerless in the face of tyranny, and hero to revenge the inequality suffered by the poor. Eric Hobsbawm's brilliant book on social bandits sums up the case for Robin Hood with the following quotations and statement:

'Man has an insatiable longing for justice. In his soul he rebels against a social order which denies it to him and whatever the world he lives in, he accuses either that social order or the entire material universe of injustice. Man is filled with a strange, stubborn urge to remember, to think things out and to change things; and in addition he carries within himself the wish to have what he cannot have—if only in the form of a fairy tale. That is perhaps the basis for the heroic sagas of all ages, all religions, all peoples and all classes.'

Including ours. That is why Robin Hood is our hero too, and will remain so.[40]

Notes

1   Quoted in J C Holt, *Robin Hood* (Thames and Hudson, 1991), p16.
2   For more about these latter day heroes, see ibid, pp62-66.
3   Ibid, p10.
4   Ibid, ch 3.
5   S Knight, *Robin Hood: a Complete Study of the English Outlaw* (Blackwells, 1994), p56.
6   Ibid, p60.
7   J C Holt, op cit, p110.
8   S Knight, op cit, p79.
9   Ibid, p80.
10   Ibid, p81.
11   C Hill, *Liberty against the Law* (Penguin Press, 1996), p76.
12   J C Holt, op cit, p40.
13   C Hill, op cit, p77.
14   Ibid, p77.
15   Ibid, p75.
16   Ibid, p87.

17   E J Hobsbawm, *Bandits* (Weidenfeld and Nicolson, 1969).
18   S Knight, op cit, p154.
19   J Ritson, *Robin Hood* (Routledge, 1997), pxi.
20   Ibid, pv.
21   S Knight, op cit, p182.
22   Ibid, p202.
23   D Underdown, *Revel, Riot and Rebellion* (Oxford Univeristy Press, 1985), p55.
24   Ibid, p45.
25   J Cox, 'Robin Hood: Myth and Reality', *Socialist Review* 148.
26   S Knight, op cit, p111.
27   D Underdown, op cit, p47.
28   Ibid, p49.
29   J C Holt, op cit, p150.
30   S Knight, op cit, p109.
31   Ibid, p109.
32   D Underdown, op cit, p282.
33   E Hobsbawm, op cit, p14.
34   Ibid, ch III.
35   Ibid, ch VIII.
36   Ibid, p54.
37   S Knight, op cit, p29.
38   E J Hobsbawm, op cit, p14.
39   For a discussion of the anti-Nazi imagery of the 1938 film, see S Knight, op cit,
      pp227-229.
40   E Hobsbawm, op cit, p115.

The vice-like hold of nationalism? A comment on Megan Trudell's 'Prelude to revolution'

IAN BIRCHALL

Megan Trudell has written an excellent account of working class opposition to the First World War.[1] Quite rightly, she focuses on the events in the latter part of the war which produced the revolutionary upsurge throughout Europe in the wake of the Russian Revolution. Yet in doing so she perhaps makes too many concessions to the conventional account of the early years of the war, referring to 'patriotic frenzy' and the 'seeming vice-like hold of nationalism', and observing that the 'outbreak of the war broke the back of the revolts' in the period immediately preceding August 1914.

In fact the picture was considerably more complex. Of course it would be naïve to deny that jingoism of the worst sort affected considerable sections of the working class—just as it would be absurd to deny that sections of the working class today are racist. But just as it would be dangerously false to write off the entire working class as racist, so too it would be quite wrong to suggest that jingoism penetrated the entire class.

In September 1914 *The Economist*, then as now the voice of the more thoughtful layer of the ruling class, reflected on the situation. While in support of the war, *The Economist* was not concerned to prove its patriotic credentials, but rather to analyse the real difficulties posed by the prosecution of the war:

Few attempts have been made to enlighten us as to the attitudes of the working classes; but it has been freely stated that in the north of England there is still a good deal of apathy. The Yorkshire newspapers, for example, are full of letters complaining bitterly that cricket and football are being continued, and that you may see 'hundreds of young fellows parading with their girls, whose ages range from 18 to 35, apparently unconcerned about those who are sacrificing everything to go to the front and fight for the honour and safety of our nation'.[2]

The article continued by quoting a letter published earlier that week in the *Yorkshire Post*:

A few days ago, in passing through one of our larger villages, I stopped to see a dozen or so young men who had joined the colours being drilled in a field. Six times as many were lying up against the fence passively looking on. I enquired of one of them, a well set-up, athletic young fellow, why he was a spectator, and not a participant. He looked at me squarely, and said: 'Because it isn't worth while; we could be no use for six months, and by that time there will be no enemy. Germany will be off the map.'

I spoke to another, who said: 'It's no business of ours, this foreign war. Austria and Servia [Serbia] should be let fight it out. Germany didn't want to come in until compelled by Russia, and we should have kept out of it; anyhow, we're all right; our fleet will keep us safe.' On the same day I saw 2,000 miners watching a great bowling match on a common. Three out of five were between the ages of 20 and 35. With difficulty I diverted the attention of a few of them from the match to the war. They spoke of it in quite a detached manner. One said we should lick the Germans, but whoever won could not do without the workers, and they would have their job anyhow. Another remarked that Kitchener had got all the men he wanted, and our fleet would starve the Germans like rats in a hole. A third said he was against the war, but now it had started let them fight it out, it made no difference to him, and so on...[3]

Such apathy was not confined to Yorkshire. In a seaside town a patriotic young woman set out to challenge all the able-bodied men she could find on the streets as to why they were not in the armed forces; she was profoundly distressed by the inadequate responses she received. She reported in a letter:

On leaving the tram-car, I asked the able-bodied young conductor if he intended to serve his country. His reply was, 'I have three brothers in the army; that's enough for me.' A little later, seeing a remarkably fine young man pushing a small laundry-cart, I asked him the same question. He replied insolently, 'I don't want to be shot!'

> *... I encountered a number of young men of all social grades. As I*
> *accosted them severally some replied indifferently, 'The Germans won't come*
> *here, no fear!' Others, again, replied, 'What about the Japanese? They will*
> *help us.' And others answered, 'There are the Russians!'*
> *... The answer of several of the young working men was, 'The gents*
> *should enlist first'.*[4]

Those of us who are sometimes distressed by the fact that football
seems to mobilise so much more energy than politics may be consoled
by the thought that it cuts both ways, as is shown by this observation
from the diary of a *Times* journalist visiting Chelsea football ground for
the game against Arsenal in December 1914:

> *In these days the posters carried by a line of sandwich-men, walking up and*
> *down before the gates of the Chelsea football ground, ask the crowd such*
> *questions as: 'Are you forgetting that there's a war on?', 'Your Country*
> *Needs You', 'Be Ready to Defend your Home and Women from the German*
> *Huns'. So far as I could notice, little attention was given to these skeletons at*
> *the feast.*[5]

Such varied expressions of a sullen and blinkered apathy are a long
way removed from proletarian internationalism, but they do show quite
clearly that 'patriotic frenzy' had not penetrated the working class as
deeply as is often believed. If any section of the left had offered a clear
internationalist lead, then it would have stood a good chance of winning
some of this section of the population to its demands. Indeed, the weakness and confusion of most of the left was a major reason why the ruling
class were able, temporarily, to win the battle of ideas. Harry McShane,
writing of the situation in Glasgow, notes that the left had not made
enough effort to explain the nature of war; recruits did not know what
they were letting themselves in for and were lulled by the claims that the
war would offer an easy victory and would last only a few weeks.[6]

In addition, despite widespread enthusiasm for the war, anti-war
activists were able to agitate in public, as shown by Ken Weller in his
excellent book *Don't be a Soldier*. The North London Herald League
held its first anti-war meeting on 5 August 1914, the day after the declaration of war, at Salisbury Corner, Harringay, and continued to hold
regular meetings.[7] Although the NLHL had only around 50 members at
the outbreak of war, it was able to grow quite rapidly within the first six
months of hostilities. One of its leading participants, R M Fox, described
the activity:

> *This anti-war activity in the early days of the war was not without its dangers,*
> *for an atmosphere of terrorisation was created. But though we got violent*

opposition, we had enthusiastic support too. Our membership mounted; from under 50 we reached a total of five or six hundred. From all over London, from the East End, from south and west, came supporters who rallied to the anti-war standard which was raised openly in Finsbury Park.[8]

Megan is quite right to point out that nationalism did not arise spontaneously, but had to be created by indoctrination on the part of the ruling class. But although nationalism had been developed over the preceding decades, the ruling class was still forced to take drastic measures during the first months of the war to create a mood of jingoistic fervour. As Megan notes, the ruling classes were not confident in advance that they could carry workers with them at the outbreak of war. In the period before 1914 there were a number of international crises—Fashoda, Morocco, Trieste—which brought Europe to the brink of war. In each case war was averted, and in each case strong anti-war feelings were manifested by the working class movement. It is true that there were forces built into the capitalist system that were pushing irresistibly towards war; in that sense war was inevitable, but there was no inevitability that war should break out in just the way it did at precisely the time it did. A strong enough response by the working class in August 1914 and war could have been postponed yet again. (Of course capitalist Europe could not achieve a state of perpetual peace, as some reformists in the Second International imagined. Sooner or later there was only one alternative to war and that was revolution.)

Those who argue that jingoism penetrated the great mass of workers have as their most fundamental argument the fact that a million workers did volunteer before the supply was exhausted and conscription was introduced in 1916. Yet the situation is not as clear cut as it might appear. The British ruling class got their volunteers, but they had to work for it. Public sensibility was inflamed by numerous unsubstantiated atrocity stories. In September 1914 the *Dumfries Standard* carried a story, soon prominently taken up by such London papers as the *Globe*, *The Star* and *The Evening Standard*, of a British nurse in Belgium who was said to have had both breasts cut off by Germans. In fact the nurse in question had never been in Belgium and the whole story had been invented by her 17 year old sister.[9] (There is nothing new under *The Sun*.) Belgium was presented as being an unfortunate victim of German imperialism,[10] largely on the basis of the fact that it looked a small country on the map. Belgium was in fact a vicious colonial power in 1914.[11]

Intense ideological struggle was conducted at every level. On 2 September a government sponsored meeting of well-known British writers was held, attended by Thomas Hardy, H G Wells, Arnold Bennett, Conan Doyle and many others, to produce a manifesto about Britain's 'destiny and duty' in the war.[12] As a result a considerable amount of patriotic prose and verse was turned out over the next four years. Above all the role of the labour leaders was crucial. In all the main combatant countries labour leaders were incorporated into the machine of the state. Their lifelong enemies in the ruling classes would not have made such offers unless they knew that the labour leaders had an indispensable role to play in mobilising their supporters.

The massive numbers of workers who volunteered in the first two years of the war must also be examined with some suspicion. Doubtless many volunteered from sincere patriotism; others from a desire for adventure or the expectation that the war would last only a few months. But many more volunteers were the victims of intimidation which went far beyond 'peer pressure' and young ladies with white feathers. Thus when 7,000 London tram workers struck for 19 days in May 1915,

> *The reaction of the London County Council (LCC), which owned the tramways, was to sack all men of military age, telling them to volunteer for the armed forces, and it issued a statement which read:*
>
> *Notice is hereby given that since the majority of men above military age have returned to work, men who are eligible for the services will not be taken back.*
>
> *a) Those who enlist will receive favourable consideration for re-employment, as far as may be possible, after the war.*
>
> *b) Any man of military age unable to enlist may appeal to the Chief Officer and state his reasons, and he will consider whether any circumstances allow any exception in his case...[13]*

In November 1915 the press reported that:

> *The prime minister's declaration that all unmarried men must serve their country has had a stimulating effect in the City. Employers who hitherto took no steps to influence the younger members of the staffs have taken action, and in many of the large City offices and warehouses a census is being taken of the eligibles, who are being asked to give to their employers reasons for not enlisting.[14]*

At the outbreak of war the Prince of Wales Fund was launched, ostensibly to relieve distress arising from the hostilities. In reality it became another means of exerting pressure to 'volunteer'. The fund:

> *...was frequently administered by charity-mongers who...were sometimes not above instituting, in relation to able bodied men of military age, their own local system of compulsory military service sanctioned by the threat of starvation.[15]*

The picture in other countries was similar: substantial support for the

war among some workers, but apathy and open resistance among others.
In Russia the Bolsheviks, who had grown enormously in strength in the
couple of years prior to the war, were able to take open and public action
against the war despite the stepping up of repression and the pro-war
hysteria which became rampant among the middle classes:

> *On the day that the army was mobilised the workers of about 20 factories*
> *struck in St Petersburg in protest against the war. In some places the workers*
> *met the reservists with shouts of, 'Down with the war', and with revolutionary*
> *songs. But the demonstrations now took place under conditions different from*
> *those of a few weeks before. The onlookers, particularly in the centre of the*
> *city, were incited by patriotic sentiment and no longer maintained a friendly*
> *neutrality, but took an active part in hunting down the demonstrators and*
> *helping the police to make arrests.*
>
> *One such 'patriotic' outburst occurred in the Nevsky Prospect on the first*
> *day of mobilisation, while a workers' demonstration was marching past the*
> *town Duma. The people in the street, mostly bourgeois loafers, who usually*
> *hid themselves or made off through side streets when workers' demonstra-*
> *tions appeared, now became very active and, with shouts of 'Traitors',*
> *assisted the police to beat up the demonstrators. The police were able to*
> *arrest the workers and take them off to the police station.*[16]

For many soldiers 'patriotic frenzy' did not survive long when confronted with the reality of the trenches. Certainly the British army
authorities felt they could not rely on the innate enthusiasm of their volunteers; it was necessary to use a mixture of indoctrination and terror to
make them fight. Executions for desertion were employed from the very
beginning of hostilities and were given maximum publicity as a matter
of policy. In September 1914 Sir Douglas Haig wrote recommending the
death sentence for a soldier who had vanished for six days when suffering shock from a shell explosion:

> *I am of the opinion that it is necessary to make an example to prevent cow-*
> *ardice in the face of the enemy as far as possible.*[17]

Those soldiers who had volunteered were not necessarily fired with a
patriotic desire to kill. On the contrary, the army training programmes
had to give systematic ideological indoctrination to recruits. British
Brigadier-General Crozier wrote of training in 1915:

> *I, for my part, do what I can to alter completely the outlook, bearing and*
> *mentality of over 1,000 men...blood lust is taught for purposes of war in*
> *bayonet fighting itself and by doping the minds of all with propagandic*

poison. The German atrocities (many of which I doubt in secret), the employment of gas in action, the violation of French women and the 'official murder' of Nurse Cavell all help to bring out the brute-like bestiality which is so necessary for victory. The process of 'seeing red', which has to be carefully cultured if the effect is to be lasting, is elaborately grafted into the makeup of even the meek and mild... The Christian churches are the finest blood lust creators which we have and of them we make free use... The British soldier is a kindly fellow... It is necessary to corrode his mentality...[18]

The Christmas truce which Megan mentions represented quite a serious threat to military discipline and the continued effective conduct of the war. In some areas the truce lasted well into January and in one section of the front it actually endured until the middle of March 1915, despite the best efforts of the army command to get the slaughter going again.[19] One letter from an army officer makes it clear that the officers on both sides shared a common interest in forcing their reluctant men to fight:

A party of unarmed Saxons continued to wander about between the lines after the prescribed time was up. They were duly warned by our men but took no notice whereupon one of our officers ordered some men to fire over them. This had no effect so a German officer sang out, 'Fire at them. I can't get the beggars in.' The English officer would not do this as they were unarmed but he rang up a battery to put a few shells over the German trench which they did, but the Saxons quite unperturbed sat down just outside our wire line and watched their pals getting shelled.[20]

In all the armed forces engaged in the war the patriotic frenzy seems to have worn off quite quickly. Thus in the German navy, seaman Richard Stumpf wrote in his diary in March 1915:

...a deep gulf has arisen between the officers and the men. The men are filled with undying hatred for the officers and the war. Everyone hopes for the return of peace. We don't even want to fight any more. We have had enough. Where is that wonderful enthusiasm of the August days?[21]

As for the working class itself, was it in the last resort nationalist or internationalist? The only answer can be: neither. Its consciousness was necessarily contradictory. As H N Brailsford noted:

Let a group of labour leaders, English and German, address a mass meeting of British working men. It can be roused to a real sense of the solidarity between the two proletariats; it can be induced to vote a contribution from its own trade union funds to assist German miners on strike; it will leave the

*meeting with a real desire for peace and fraternity between the two nations...
The same crowd, prepared by the press and artfully stimulated by skilful
orators, could also be induced to applaud the speeches of naval scaremongers,
and to go away shouting for more dreadnoughts, and looking for
German airships in the sky.*[22]

Brailsford seems to see the working class in rather too passive terms,
but basically he is right. Both alternatives were potentially present; political
struggle would decide which came out on top. In 1914 the reformists
betrayed and the internationalists were defeated. But, as Brecht once
pointed out, the only lesson of defeat is that we should do better next
time.

I think, therefore, that Megan has tended to overestimate the grip of
nationalism in the first six or nine months of the war. This is not simply
a question of historical pedantry. The implications of the argument about
the early phase of the war have vital relevance. As Megan shows, it was
at the end of the war that the working class was strong enough to build
the mass parties of the Comintern. But if world war ever recurs we shall
not have the opportunity to wait till the end. In a nuclear world, revolution
must precede and not follow war.

The year 1914 was a catastrophic defeat for the left. The capitulation
of the reformists had deep roots in their previous history. Even the best
of the revolutionary left, the Bolsheviks, despite their political clarity
and organisational roots, could not prevent their rulers from plunging
into war.

Whether things could have turned out differently can only be a matter
of speculation. What is certain is that the working class did not unanimously
embrace war with enthusiasm, even in the opening months
before the realities of trench warfare became apparent. From the first
days there were counter-currents which enabled genuine internationalists
to start a fightback. Nationalism is a powerful and poisonous force, but it
is not invincible.

Notes
1   M Trudell, 'Prelude to Revolution: Class Consciousness and the First World War',
      International Socialism 76, pp67-107.
2   *The Economist*, 5 September 1914.
3   *Yorkshire Post*, 2 September 1914.
4   A M B Meakin, *Enlistment or Conscription* (London, 1915), pp10-11, cited in D
      Hayes, *Conscription Conflict* (London, 1949), pp165-166.
5   M MacDonagh, *In London during the Great War* (London, 1935), p44.
6   H McShane, *No Mean Fighter* (London, 1978), pp61-63.
7   K Weller, *Don't be a Soldier: the Radical Anti-War Movement in North London
      1914-1918* (London, 1985), p37.
8   R M Fox, *Smoky Crusade* (London, 1937), cited in K Weller, op cit, p38.
9   A Ponsonby, *Falsehood in War-Time* (London, 1928), pp67-70.

10 Of course there were genuine atrocities—committed by all sides. Thus the Germans were accused, with some justice, of executing Belgian civilians. The Germans in turn claimed that the 'civilians' were in fact guerrilla troops.

11 The Belgian Congo (now Democratic Republic of Congo) was the personal property of King Leopold II until 1908, when he made it over to Belgium. Colonial rule was marked by forced labour, torture and massacre.

12 D G Wright, 'The Great War, Government Propaganda and English "Men of Letters" 1914-16', *Literature and History* no 7 (1978), pp70-100.

13 K Weller, op cit, p29.

14 *Enfield Gazette and Observer*, 19 November 1915.

15 R Harrison, 'The War Emergency Workers' National Committee 1914-1920', in A Briggs and J Saville (eds), *Essays in Labour History 1886-1923* (London, 1971), p235.

16 A Y Badeyev, *Bolsheviks in the Tsarist Duma* (London, 1987), p199.

17 A Babington, *For the Sake of Example* (London, 1983), pp7, 29.

18 F P Crozier, *A Brass Hat in No-Man's-Land* (London, 1930), p42; cited by T H Wintringham, *Mutiny* (London, 1936), pp308-309.

19 M Brown and S Seaton, *Christmas Truce* (London, 1994), pp182-185.

20 Ibid, p168.

21 D Horn (ed), *War, Mutiny and Revolution in the German Navy: The World War I Diary of Richard Stumpf* (New Brunswick, NJ, 1967), p75. Stumpf, a Catholic, nationalist, conservative who served as an ordinary seaman throughout the First World War, kept a diary which is a remarkable document of the ebbs and flows of class consciousness. In June 1917 he wrote: 'As a good German and as a Catholic, I hope that we might emerge from this war with a total victory... From the opposite point of view everything is different. Then I am not a German but a proletarian, and as such, I hope for a great, but not an annihilating defeat. Why should I feel this way? Past experience tells me that the lower classes stand to benefit from a defeat while the rich stand to lose. I cannot conceive of the achievements of the Young Turk Revolution without the background of the battles of Plevna and Shipka Pass.' There could be no better proof than the testimony of the good conservative Stumpf that Lenin's strategy of 'revolutionary defeatism' could reach the consciousness of the masses.

22 Cited in H B Davis, *Nationalism and Socialism* (New York, 1973), pp112-113.

In perspective: Alexander Cockburn and Christopher Hitchens

WILLIAM KEACH

Alexander Cockburn and Christopher Hitchens are among a handful of writers based in the US whose regular columns, articles and books offer sustained leftist criticism of Clinton's America. Whatever the limits of their contribution to building a serious political alternative, Cockburn and Hitchens have done much to keep thoughtful, at times radical, analysis and resistance alive in a period when American liberalism and social democracy offer little but defensive capitulation to Clintonism.

Radical journalists: from Britain to the US

Cockburn and Hitchens began their careers as Oxford educated radicals and precocious London based journalists. Cockburn grew up in Ireland: his father was the well known Communist Party activist and writer Claud Cockburn. Hitchens described his background as 'very naval, military, and conservative': his father was a naval officer based in Portsmouth. Hitchens was 'the first member of my family ever to go to private school or even to university'.[1]

Cockburn worked at the *Times Literary Supplement* for two years in the mid-1960s, then at *New Left Review* and *The New Statesman*. He co-edited volumes published by Penguin on the trade unions and the student movement before moving to the US in 1973, at a time when the gruesome war in South East Asia was finally winding down and the movements of the 1960s were losing steam. Hitchens, who is some seven years younger, was already reviewing for *The New Statesman* as a student at Balliol College, Oxford. After he graduated, Balliol gave him a scholarship to travel in the US. He returned to London and a job on the *Times Higher Education Supplement*, then he published a little book on Marx and the Paris Commune and, at the age of 22, was offered a job on the staff of *The New Statesman*. His professional friends at that time, he says, were Martin Amis, Julian Barnes, James Fenton and Timothy Noel:

> *I realised these guys were better at* [writing fiction] *than I was. It was rather intimidating that they were so good. It made me specialise more in the generalist-type political essay. But they were very good people to work with, for style. They persuaded me it wasn't enough just to make the point: that style **was** substance.*[2]

Hitchens brought this attitude with him when he moved to the US in the early 1980s.

Cockburn and Hitchens are best known now to US readers through their columns in *The Nation*, a fortnightly magazine with a largish subscription ('One American in 2,559 subscribes to *The Nation*' reads their current internal ad) and a political spectrum that runs from mainstream Democratic Party liberal to social democratic. Cockburn's 'Beat the Devil' column, which has appeared in *The Nation* since 1984, stands significantly outside this spectrum, in ways that I'll discuss more fully later on. Cockburn wrote regularly for the *Village Voice* for many years, and throughout the 1980s appeared as licensed radical on the opinions page of the *Wall Street Journal*. Now he writes a nationally syndicated column for the *Los Angeles Times* and is a regular contributor to the *New York Review of Books*, *Atlantic*, *Harper's*, and *In These Times*. His books include *Corruptions of Empire* (1987), *The Fate of the Forest: Developers, Destroyers, and Defenders of the Amazon* (1989, with Susan Hecht), *The Golden Age is in Us* (1995), and the brilliant *Washington Babylon* (1996, with Ken Silverstein). In 1996 he and Silverstein launched *CounterPunch*, a superb six to ten page muckraker that 'Tells the facts and names the names' twice monthly.

Hitchens's column in *The Nation*, 'Minority Report', began running in 1982. He has also served as Washington editor of *Harper's* and as book critic for the New York paper *Newsday*, and he is a regular contributor to the *London Review of Books*, *Granta*, *New Left Review*, *Dissent*, as well as to such expensive, yuppy-chic magazines as *Vogue* and *Vanity Fair* (his column in the latter is called '*Fin de Siècle*'). In addition to his early book on the Paris Commune, Hitchens is the author of *Callaghan: The Road to Number Ten* (1976), *Hostage to History: Cyprus from the Ottomans to Kissinger* (1989, scheduled to be reissued by Verso in the autumn), *Imperial Spoils: The Case of the Parthenon Marbles* (1989), *Blood, Class, and Nostalgia: Anglo-American Ironies* (1990), *The Missionary Position: Mother Theresa in Theory and Practice* (1995). Many of his columns and articles are collected in *Prepared for the Worst* (1989) and *For the Sake of Argument* (1993). In 1988 he co-edited with Edward Said and also contributed to an excellent volume published by Verso called *Blaming the Victims: Spurious Scholarship and the Palestinian Question.*

Muckraking and stylish exposé

To think about Cockburn and Hitchens is to realise just how much political muck there is to be raked through these days in the US. Nobody does this kind of journalistic work with more fearless tenacity and sharper wit than Cockburn. In one issue of *The Nation* Cockburn exposed why his editors had reduced his regular column. Right wingers have 'chided me in the past for being keener to attack the Clinton crowd than Newt and his gang', Cockburn notes, and:

> *Navasky and vanden Heuvel [**The Nation**'s editors] taxed me with the same supposed sin a few months before the 96 election, when the All-Out-For-Bill drive was in full spate. Well, there's no keener pleasure in life than giving liberal pretensions a sound kick in the backside, and besides, a lot of the enduring damage is done by liberals and by the liberal culture of which this magazine—which Navasky and vanden Heuvel carefully call 'independent' rather than 'left'—is an increasingly sedulous exponent.*[3]

This kind of feisty independence from his own editors and from what the US mainstream regards as 'the left' gives Cockburn's voice its distinctive polemical edge. He goes on in this column to defend a journalist who has just been sacked from *In These Times* (another left-liberal magazine with smaller circulation that *The Nation*) for daring to 'raise the name of Leon Trotsky'; to ridicule Martin Walker, US bureau chief of *The Guardian*, for being 'a sycophant in the Clinton Court from the start' and for his disgusting praise of Secretary of State Madeleine Albright's policy towards Iraq; and to continue an exposure of recent censorship at another hallowed liberal institution, Pacifica Radio. Cockburn concludes the last of his two page 'Beat the Devils' with splendid sarcasm:

> *As you can see, such sagas indicate that the whole non-profit third sector that underwrites liberalism in America is marking out the limits of permissible discourse. Welcome to a political culture defined by the MacArthur Foundation, the Rockefeller Family Fund, the Pew Charitable Trust, the Ford*

Foundation, the Carnegie Endowment... [liberals] *called for bold new thinking and fresh ideas, just like that Clinton clone Tony Blair, now pledging to honour Tory budgets, Tory schedules of privatisation, the Thatcherite agenda more or less in toto, all under the approving endorsement of Rupert Murdoch. But dear me! I see I'm overshooting even the two page limit. Sorry to run on so. It won't happen again.*

Cockburn specialises in uncompromising denunciations of liberals and soft-leftists who try to defend themselves in *The Nation*'s Letters column from his attacks. When Patricia Scott, executive director of Pacifica Radio, writes to defend her organisation's commitment to 'alternative viewpoints, freedom of the press', Cockburn replies with, 'Don't make me laugh... Gag orders and secret board meetings...should not be procedures associated with public radio'.[4] Many a *Nation* reader over the years has written in to protest at Cockburn's unmannerly assault on his or her favourite liberal or social democratic intellectual or politician, only to have Cockburn respond with a savage refusal to be nice.

The best of Cockburn's recent work as muckraker and gadfly is to be found in *Washington Babylon*. The obvious pleasure Cockburn takes in his role as maverick journalist seems to enable, rather than impede, his collaborative research and writing with Ken Silverstein, both in this book and in *Counterpunch*. *Washington Babylon* specifically targets the national press and media establishment, the Congress, the lobbyists, the presidency—those key institutions of ruling class power and manipulation that most Americans rightly see as corrupt. 'Both major political parties', Cockburn and Silverstein say in their introduction,

have been bought up by big money from corporations and wealthy Americans... More than 100 corporate political actions committees contribute to both 'liberal Democrat' Richard Gephardt and 'right wing Republican' Newt Gingrich. Never have Tweedledee and Tweedledum been so indistinguishable.[5]

Quoting Hal Draper's famous article, 'Who's Going to be the Lesser Evil in 1968?', Cockburn and Silverstein show that Draper's argument against the politics of 'lesser evilism' in 1968 applies even more decisively to the US today. Democratic Party politicians widely believed to offer a respectable alternative to Clintonian sleaze are revealed as offering no such thing. Recently retired Senator Bill Bradley of New Jersey fought long and hard to defend the interests of the huge drug companies based in his state. That he did so is not surprising: 'The pharmaceutical industry spends about $10 billion a year on advertising and promotion'.[6] In 1993, when Clinton himself proposed to make the government the sole buyer of childhood vaccines and to distribute them free to all children, it was Bradley who led the successful fight against this reform—despite the fact that US drug companies have raised vaccine prices by 1,000 percent in the last 15 years, and that fewer than two thirds of two year old children receive the full spectrum of recommended immunisations. It's this kind of analysis and exposure, aimed at politicians and institutions who tend to evade widespread public anger, that makes *Washington Babylon*, and Cockburn's writing generally, important.

Hitchens too can be an effective muckraker. In a 'Minority Report' column from April 1997, for example, he exposes the crimes of Jacques Foccart, the Gaullist 'destabliser, the assassin, the paymaster and the procurer for the French neo-colonies' in Zaire and other French dominated African countries.[7] *For the Sake of Argument* contains good pieces from the late 1980s and early 1990s—like 'Befriending the Kurds', in which Hitchens surveys the appalling history of US promises to and betrayals of these stateless and beleaguered people.[8] 'Songs Fit for Heroes' is based on Hitchens's access to 'the recreational songbook of the 77th Tactical Fighter Squadron of the United States Air Force, based at Upper Heyford' just outside Oxford. One of the less offensive verses Hitchens quotes from this noble document runs as follows:

Phantom flyers in the sky,
Persian-pukes prepare to die.
Rolling in with snake and nape,
Allah creates but we cremate.

Hitchens notes that the songbook attributes one of its stirring quotations to a famous Nazi Luftwaffe pilot.[9]

But Hitchens's preferred mode is the scandalous personal encounter narrative or review essay, rather than the detailed investigative excavation into the squalid brutalities of mainstream politics. In his regular pieces for the *London Review of Books* he lets the author in question produce the muck—then he comes in with his sardonic wit. Such is the case in a review in February 1997 of a book by Clinton's scandalously discredited former campaign adviser, Dick Morris:

*I was travelling in Illinois when I first heard some beefy local pol utter the profound post-modern truth that 'politics is showbiz for ugly people'. Yes, you too may be a mediocre, flaky-scalped, pudgy sycophant. But, with the right 'skills', you also can possess a cellular phone and keep a limo on call and 'take meetings' and issue terse directives like 'I want this **yesterday**, understand.' Unfortunately, the women you meet in the politics biz will tend to be rather too much like yourself. But, hey, bimbos can be rented! And won't they*

*just be impressed to death when you pass them the bedroom telephone exten-
sion and it's the Prez talking.*[10]

This is characteristic Hitchens prose, full of funny turns that derive
their energy from a disgusted fascination with the sordid world he paro-
dies. Where Cockburn usually writes at a serious literal and critical
distance from this world, Hitchens writes much more from inside it, up
close to it. A recent *London Review of Books* account of John Davis's
Intimate Memoir of Jacqueline Kennedy Onassis begins like this:

> The *44* Restaurant in the Royalton Hotel at 44 West 44th Street is a pretty suave
> and worldly Manhattan lunchery. So at any rate it seems to my provincial,
> country mouse Washingtonian optic. I am sometimes taken there for a treat by
> my editors at **Conde Nast**, who use the place as a sort of staff canteen.[11]

Hitchens likes to be the left journalist with the Bailliol pedigree who
gets invited to places like the Royalton Hotel and then reveals how
corrupt they are.

But if the manner and stance of Hitchens's journalism is often snob-
bish and self-regarding, its political substance is often worth taking
seriously. Like Cockburn, he is an articulate Clinton hater. A piece last
summer entitled 'A Hard Dog to Keep on the Porch' does a superb job of
linking Clinton's repellant lack of personal integrity to his success as a
politician on whom much of the US ruling class can rely.[12] Sometimes,
however, Hitchens takes up the right side of the right cause on a less than
fully informed basis. In his 'Minority Report' for *The Nation* of 31
March, 1997 Hitchens summarises the most recent efforts by the state of
Pennsylvania to execute former Black Panther Mumia Abu-Jamal, but
only after declaring that he was 'not prepared to say for certain that I
think this defendant is innocent as charged'.[14] In his next column,
Hitchens had to acknowledge that his neutrality on the question of guilt
or innocence had been based on his not knowing that the prosecution had
been unable to prove that Mumia had fired the revolver in his possession
on the night of the murder of a Philadelphia police officer, or that the
calibre of Mumia's gun was 38mm, not 44mm like that of the bullet
recovered from the policeman's body.[15] In Hitchens' journalism, political
positions are sometimes as much a matter of striking the desired posture
as of arguing from the available evidence.

Underlying politics: commitments and evasions

Looking beyond Cockburn's and Hitchens' week to week journalistic
performances to their deeper political attitudes and commitments is not a
straightforward matter. In capitalist society today—and nowhere more

deceptively than in the US—journalists are expected to maintain a stance of professional 'independence' and 'objectivity', if not neutrality. 'Radical' journalists in particular are tolerated and accorded some degree of credibility only as long as they don't openly identify themselves with an organised movement or party. This means that whatever broader allegiances they might hold or be inclined to advance, Cockburn and Hitchens have much more freedom to produce muckraking criticism and satire than they do to contribute towards building an identifiable political alternative.

This being said, it's not clear just what sort of political alternative they think the rest of us should be building. Cockburn's personal history links him to the politics of the Communist Party, and there are still moments in his writing—debating the number of people estimated to have perished in Stalin's gulags, claiming that 'the Brezhnev years were a Golden Age for the Soviet working class',[16] when aspects of his father's convictions can be glimpsed. But these days Cockburn conveys few illusions in, and no nostalgia for, the Communist Party and the Soviet Union. He sometimes writes openly as a Marxist, but as a Marxist with no positive and overarching political project in view. He consistently supports the rebuilding of the trade union movement and is passionately committed to defending the environment from corporate devastation, but he sees no larger political initiative that can connect and eventually achieve these objectives. Cockburn's relation to Marxism is partial and, ultimately, contradictory: it grounds his fearless and revealing critique of capitalist society but provides no practical direction for even the beginnings of an organised counterforce.

All of this is evident in Cockburn's *The Golden Age is in Us*, published by Verso in 1996. To be fair, the book is subtitled *Journeys & Encounters* and offers informal reminiscences, journal sketches, and conversations rather than sustained argument or analysis. Yet even reading the book on its own terms, one is struck by how little attention Cockburn gives to the prospects for a coherent and relevant Marxist politics today. In a series of entries responding to the 1991 coup attempt against Gorbachev and the imminent collapse of the Soviet Union Cockburn comes closest to assessing the prospects for Marxism. Cockburn's journal entries from late August 1991 reflect a lingering, half hearted attachment to the idea that some form of real, if flawed, communism was in its death throes. He quotes Lenin as saying in 1917:

> 'One can never be radical enough; that is, one must always try to be as radical as reality itself.'
> That last line has always been one of my favorites, and I hope to be using it long after the last bust of the man Reagan insisted on calling Nokolai has

been ground down to talcum powder.[17]

The trouble is that Cockburn understands Lenin's maxim through a
historical perspective distorted by Stalinist myth. Consider the following:

> *The Soviet Union defeated Hitler and fascism. Without it, the Cuban
> Revolution would never have survived, nor the Vietnamese. In the post-war
> years it was the counterweight to US imperialism and the terminal savageries
> of the old European colonial powers. It gave support to any country trying to
> follow an independent line. Without it, just such a relatively independent
> country as India could instead have taken a far more rightward course.
> Despite Stalin's suggestion to Mao that he and his comrades settle for only
> half a country, the Chinese Revolution probably would not have survived
> either.*[18]

Every sentence of this paragraph belies Cockburn's political intelli-
gence and represents a barrier to his asking the most important political
questions. In what sense had either the Cuban or the Vietnamese revolutions survived by 1991? Was the Soviet Union a 'counterweight to US
imperialism' or a rival imperialist power in its own right, imposing its
own regimes of repression? Did the Soviet Union encourage or block the
development of genuine socialist politics in India? Caught up in the terminal crisis of Stalinist Russia, and obviously appalled by a world
increasingly dominated by US style market capitalism, Cockburn
retreats to a backward looking defence of mythical Russian accomplish-
ments.

Cockburn clearly felt in August of 1991 that the world had entered the
era of 'post-communism'. Just where this left him politically is indicated
by his quoting a from Vietnamese intellectual Nguyen Khac Vien: 'If a
world front of capital is being founded, its counterweight, the democratic
popular front on a world scale, is also in formation'.[19] This is where
Cockburn was left by the collapse of the Soviet Union, with a nebulous
global popular frontism.

It may still be where he would position himself today, were he to
speak explicitly about his broader principles and perspectives. But
what's striking about *The Golden Age is in Us* is that Cockburn's friends
and correspondents are often more open about their political principles
than he is. Consider the case of Cockburn's friend Frank Bardacke.
Bardacke raised key points in response to Cockburn's column in an
admirably straightforward way:

> *My own view is that the key error was the substitution of the party for the
> working class as the agent of history... Lenin's idea of the party was too
> undemocratic to nurture a revolutionary movement from the bottom. It was*

good for seizing power, but not for building revolutionary working class power. Trotsky later in his life, sometime in the 1930s, put it like this: 'The Dictatorship of the Proletariat becomes the Dictatorship of the Party becomes the Dictatorship of the Central Committee becomes the Dictatorship of the Dictator.'... But if a Leninist party cannot nurture real revolutionary power among the people in a post-revolutionary world, we are in a bad fix. Because it seems very hard to achieve the first steps in a revolution (seizing state power) without one. I don't know what to say to this.

There is of course much to say in response to Bardacke's letter, about the relative size of the Russian working class between 1917 and the end of the civil war as it shaped the character and direction of the Bolshevik Party; about the savagery of the counter-revolution and the foreign invasions; about the failure of socialist revolutions to seize state power in Germany and elsewhere in Europe; about the eventual economic and political structure of a society which continued to call itself 'socialist' but was run by a privileged bureaucracy that is now busily accommodating itself to the brutality of market capitalism. But Cockburn says nothing about any of this. His friend's questions, speculations, and worries are left hanging: no response, no agreement or disagreement, no answers.

Cockburn's failure to comment on Bardacke's quoting of Trotsky is symptomatic. 'Robin [Blackburn] sends me a good quote from Trotsky,' he writes in an earlier journal entry (17 April 1990), and then gives the rest of the entry over to a passage from *The Revolution Betrayed* in which Trostky considers two hypotheses: one, 'that the Soviet bureaucracy is overthrown by a revolutionary party having all the attributes of old Bolshevism'; two, that 'a bourgeois party were to overthrow the ruling Soviet caste'. Trotsky concludes that in the second case, such a bourgeois party 'would find no small number of ready servants among the present bureaucrats, administrators, technicians, directors, party secretaries and privileged upper circles...a bourgeois restoration would probably have to clean out fewer people than a revolutionary party'.[20] Cockburn gives no indication of what he finds 'good' about Trotsky's assessment. The initial judgment is encouraging, but the subsequent silence is significant, since it bears critically on Cockburn's whole attitude towards the former Soviet Union and 'actually existing socialism'.

Again and again in *The Golden Age is in Us* Cockburn poses questions fundamental to the rebuilding of a serious socialist alternative but refuses to stay for, or even entertain, a plausible socialist answer. In *Washington Babylon* he and Ken Silverstein embrace Hal Draper's classic attack on the politics of 'lesser evilism' but advance no specific case for a broad based, organised response to the oppression and corruption they uncover. The gesture towards global popular frontism of 1991 survives in Cockburn's lingering attraction to populist politics: in 1992 he supported former California Governor Jerry Brown's call for a flat tax to replace the graduated income tax; he praises his California friend Bruce Anderson, 1994 candidate for Fifth District Supervisor in Mendocino County, as 'a socialist in the populist style'; he admires Senator Paul Wellstone of Minnesota as a 'principled populist'.[21] The sense of class division and class struggle that usually informs Cockburn's journalism fades into the background the closer he gets to addressing the fundamental question of political organisation and rebuilding the left in the US.

While Cockburn's political past is rooted in Communist Party politics, Hitchens was involved during the late 1960s and early 1970s with the International Socialists (forerunner of the Socialist Workers Party in Britain). And while Cockburn tends these days to be vague and elusive about his general view of Marxist politics, Hitchens comments more readily—usually with an air of knowing cynicism and condescension—on his youthful membership in the IS and on the current status of revolutionary socialism.

'In the Bright Autumn of my Senescence' is the title Hitchens gave to a piece published in the *London Review of Books* on 6 January 1994—ostensibly a review of *In the Heat of the Struggle: Twenty-Five Years of Socialist Worker* and of Paul Foot's *Why You Should Join the Socialists*. The basic narrative pattern of this piece is familiar in the autobiographies of former left activists. Disgusted by the war in Vietnam and the Labour government's support for it, Hitchens was drawn to the IS when he was a student at Oxford because of its commitment to principled and open minded Marxist analysis and to concrete interventions in the class struggle wherever and whenever opportunities presented themselves. In 1968 he saw the group grow in size and confidence, the name of its paper change from *Labour Worker* to *Socialist Worker*, its links with the organised working class expand and deepen. But in the course of the 1970s, as the IS developed into the SWP (and as Hitchens began his travels in the US and his career as a full time journalist), he claims to have found his chosen party less open to intellectual debate, more inclined to opportunistic interventions and to misguided support for workers' revolutionary self-activity (Portugal in 1975). So, with an 'empty feeling', he 'quietly cancelled my membership and did a fade'.

Most of the historical points Hitchens attempts to make about the political development of the IS/SWP were effectively countered by Chris Harman and others who wrote in to the *London Review of Books*. There is more to say, though, about how this piece reflects upon Hitchens' current politics. When he considers the collection of articles from *Socialist Worker*, Hitchens finds a great falling off from the days when he himself was 'features editor' of the paper:

Most of the stuff is pure 'filler', principally made up of exhortation and, of that exhortation, principally composed of crude syndicalist diatribe. Here is a record of strikes that didn't come off, and of strikes that did while failing to make any difference.[22]

The problem here is not simply that Hitchens offers no commentary on any particular strike or industrial dispute from the 25 years covered by *In the Heat of the Struggle*. It is that Hitchens's judgment is totally disconnected from the shifting political landscape through the 1970s and 1980s into the early 1990s, and from any concrete alternative perspective on how a socialist organisation that takes its work seriously ought to have related to and represented efforts by workers during these years to fight back against both the rising and waning tide of Thatcherism. Turning to Paul Foot's *Why You Should Join the Socialists*, Hitchens is offended by Foot's claim that 'the economic and social system called capitalism' is 'run entirely by vampires': 'Not only does it make me cringe to read this in the bright autumn of my senescence, it would have made me cringe to read it when I was 17 or 18 and first started going to socialist meetings.'[23]

Cringing comes easily to Hitchens. If he cringes at Foot's use of a familiar and popular Gothic caricature, presumably he cringes—and cringed back in his hot socialist youth—at Marx's attack in his inaugural address to the First International on capitalists opposed to the Ten Hour Bill: 'British industry...vampire like, could but live by sucking blood, and children's blood'.[24] Or at Marx's argument in the *Grundrisse* that 'capital obtains this ability [to incarnate itself in fleeting commodities and take on their form] only by constantly sucking in living labour as its soul, vampire like'.[25] It's not just that Hitchens keeps a fastidious distance between himself and traditional socialist ways of imaging capitalist exploitation. It's that he conveys no sympathy of any kind with the conviction that capitalism is a monstrous system, that it survives by parasitically appropriating living labour.

At the centre of Hitchens's critical account of the international socialist movement is his belief that it has turned politically from Luxemburg towards Lenin. 'The essential precepts descended from Luxemburg rather than Lenin,' he writes in the *London Review of Books* article about 'the group' he joined in the late 1960s, but by 1975 the SWP's response to the Portugese Revolution showed that 'the comrades' had 'moved from Luxemburg to the worst of Lenin'.[26] The counterposing of Luxemburg and Lenin, the celebration of the former over the latter, is a familiar move by those who don't want to come to grips with the hard practical questions of what it means to build a revolutionary party. More importantly, it distorts both the significant points of debate between Lenin and Luxemburg and the areas of fundamental and lasting agreement. You would never know from reading Hitchens, for example, that Luxemburg came to agree with Lenin on the necessity of building a revolutionary party, or that Lenin celebrates Luxemburg's criticism of German leftist 'parliamentarianism' in *'Left Wing' Communism—an Infantile Disorder* (1920).

The evasions and confusions in Hitchens's account of his own relation to revolutionary socialist politics are relevant to what is sometimes disappointing in his journalistic writing. Consider, in this regard, a quite recent and extended piece in *The New York Review of Books* on Che Guevara. Hitchens does an effective job of distinguishing Guevara's real political motivations and activities from the superficial exploitation of his popularity by interests ranging from the Cuban Ministry of Tourism to Sir Andrew Lloyd Webber. When it comes to assessing Guevara's politics, however, Hitchens has recourse to the same misrepresentations of the Marxist political tradition that he relies on in rationalising his own history. To undermine the credibility of Guevara's defence of improvised tribunals and executions during the Cuban Revolution ('Look, in this thing either you kill first, or else you get killed,' he is quoted as having said to a former medical colleague), Hitchens cites Guevara's belief in 'democratic centralism' and scoffs at Guevara's favouring Lenin over Luxemburg on the question of internal party organisation.[27] In his discussion of 'democratic centralism' not a word is said about the class forces involved in the Cuban Revolution—about the fundamental differences between the Bolshevik Party in Russia of 1917 and the force that succeeded in overthrowing the Batista regime in Cuba in 1959. It's this lack of clarity in basic political perspective that leads Hitchens on to a fatuous comparison between Guevara's later political work and 'Trotsky in exile', and then to the defeatist conclusion that 'the very element that gave [Guevara] his certainty and courage—his revolutionary communism—was also the element that condemned him to historical eclipse'.[28] No wonder this article is titled 'Goodbye to All That'.

Radical journalists and the fight for a socialist alternative

Hitchens and Cockburn offer something rare in US journalism these days—a spirited left wing analysis of the ongoing ravages of US imperialism, of the growing economic inequality in the world's richest nation, of the falling living standards for most workers, of the massive corruption from the top to the bottom of the political system. That they are able to provide this analysis for a national and international readership at a time when the US left remains weak and fragmented is extremely important. In the midst of the recent successful strike by the Teamsters against United Parcel Service, it was wonderful to see Cockburn returning to the opinions page of *The Wall Street Journal* (14 August 1997) and fiercely defending the union's decision to take on one of the wealthiest and most politically powerful corporations in the country. But what does it mean that Cockburn was given this opportunity by one of the bosses' premier media giants—by a newspaper that for months had been conducting an attack on the Teamsters and its president, Ron Carey? Would the *Wall Street Journal* have printed Cockburn's piece if it had linked the UPS strike and the revival of the US labour movement explicitly to the project of building a militantly anti-capitalist, pro-worker socialist party in the US?

The constraints and limitations I'm talking about are not entirely a matter of what the capitalist press will and will not allow to appear in its profitable pages. In their distinctive ways, Cockburn and Hitchens delight in their roles as rogue journalists, as displaced mavericks from Britain who are allowed to entertain as well as inform and provoke their readers by taking a caustic look at a ruling class more than confident enough (at the moment) to tolerate such 'freedom of the press'. At the same time, there is a peculiarly American tradition of independent radical journalism that has made possible, in Cockburn's case more than in Hitchens's, the fashioning of a not altogether unfamiliar identity and career. In many respects the model for *CounterPunch* is *I F Stone's Weekly*, despite Cockburn's critical comments on Stone near the beginning of *The Golden Age is in Us*. Stone, an intrepid civil libertarian, revealed a lot of ruling class dirt and brutality in his day, and in the process certainly gave encouragement to movements on the left. But even during the Vietnam War Stone didn't contribute substantially to the building of an organisation, party, or movement. And he was certainly not a Marxist.

Do Cockburn and Hitchens think of themselves as Marxists? Cockburn does, I believe; Hitchens probably doesn't. The point to emphasise is that in Cockburn's case as well as in Hitchens's, the crucial link in Marxist politics between analysis and practice, between critical participation in a society and militant intervention to transform that society, has been attenuated and in some respects broken. Of course radical journalism itself is a form of practice and intervention. But such journalism can never meet the test of a genuine Marxist politics as long as it holds itself aloof from organising a movement and building a party.

To give a critical assessment of Cockburn's and Hitchens's broader political perspectives, particularly of their often averted and defensive relation to any kind of organised socialist politics, is by no means to minimise the importance of their work as journalists. Nor is it to overlook the practical pressures on professional jouralists operating today in the US—or in other countries for that matter. It is instead to make clear how distant even the best radical journalism in the US is from the project of mobilising political power from below according to a consistent socialist analysis and set of organising principles and objectives. Socialists have long read Cockburn and Hitchens with interest and admiration. We will no doubt continue to do so. But we should take every opportunity to argue with them, to make the case that the best contributions to coming struggles will be made by members of the best revolutionary socialist party workers can build.

Notes

1   Interview with Sasha Abramsky in *The Progressive*, February 1997, p32.
2   Ibid, p34.
3   *The Nation*, 5 May 1997, pp9-10.
4   *The Nation*, 9 June 1997, p23.
5   A Cockburn and K Silverstein, *Washington Babylon* (London, 1996), p ix.
6   Ibid, p99.
7   *The Nation*, 28 April 1997, p9.
8   C Hitchens, *For the Sake of Argument*, pp89-91; the piece originally appeared in *The Nation*, May 1991.
9   Ibid, pp96-98; originally in *The Nation*, February 1989.
10   C Hitchens, 'Bill and Dick's Excellent Adventure' (a review of D Morris, *Behind the Oval Office: Winning the Presidency in the Nineties), London Review of Books*, 20 February 1997, p25.
11   C Hitchens, 'National Treasure', *London Review of Books*, 14 November 1996, pp19-20.
12   *London Review of Books*, 6 June 1996, pp3-7.
13   *Vanity Fair*, March 1997, pp88-96.
14   *The Nation*, 31 March 1997, p8.
15   *The Nation*, 14 April 1997, p8.
16   A Cockburn, *The Golden Age is in Us: Journeys & Encounters (*London, 1996), p226.
17   Ibid, p225.
18   Ibid, p226.
19   Ibid, p227-228. The reference in this entry to Claud Cockburn's memoir is as follows: 'My father often talked to me about the If Only fallacy. Discussing the pact between the Soviet Union and Germany in 1939, he wrote in his memoir, *Crossing the Line*, "Nobody can judge whether an historical event, an order to an army, a diplomatic manoeuvre, was a catastrophe or otherwise unless he is prepared to say at the same time what *would* have happened if that thing had *not* happened. And since nobody is in a position honestly to make such a statement about what the alternative would have been, the question is in the nature of things unanswerable and otiose.'
20   Ibid, p242.
21   Ibid, p401. For Cockburn's work with University of California economist Robert Pollin in support of a flat tax proposal, see *The Golden Age is in Us*, pp281-282. For Cockburn on Wellstone, see *The Nation*, 25 November 1996, p9. See also

Cockburn's 1988 journal entry on the American Populist Party in 1892: 'With the end of the Populists came [quoting Lawrence Goodwyn] "the last substantial effort at a structural alteration of hierarchical economic forms in modern America"' (*The Golden Age is in Us*, pp48-49). In response to a recent question submitted through the 'Ask Alex' news group on the '*Nation* On Line', Cockburn replied, 'Not sure what you mean by socialism from below. These days, I'm heading into redneck populism I suppose.' Thanks to Anthony Arnove for this last reference.

22 Ibid, p18.
23 Ibid, p18.
24 K Marx (edited by D Fernbach), *The First International and After: Political Writings*, ed. David Fernbach (Penguin, 1974), III, p79.
25 K Marx, *Grundrisse* (Penguin, 1973), p646.
26 *London Review of Books*, 6 January 1994, p18.
27 *The New York Review of Books*, 17 July 1997, p22.
28 Ibid, p23.

New video

Marxism

THE EVENT

Marxism 97 now out on video

'Socialism and democracy'—is the left on the rise?

'The first of May and the size of the Labour majority shows how much people in this country want change. But the Labour government has absolutely committed itself to Tory spending plans. At some point in the future there will be a clash and that will erupt in strikes'

■TRADE UNIONIST filmed at Marxism 97

On 1 May a new Labour government was elected with a landslide majority, and there has been renewed union and left wing political activity across Europe.

But what is the real importance of these events to socialists in Britain today? What is the relationship between socialism and democracy and how much can be achieved for socialism through parliamentary means?

A new video explores these issues at the Marxism 97 conference, the leading event in left wing politics.

Paul Foot, Lindsey German and Tony Benn speak on the most crucial issues facing the left today.

The video also features trade unionist and left wing activists from all over Britain. They speak frankly about the pressures they face in the workplace, their feelings about New Labour, and their hopes for the future.

Video running time: 55 minutes

£12, plus £1 postage and packing

To buy a copy of the Marxism 97 video, send a cheque for £13 to Norman Thomas, TV Choice, 22 Charing Cross Road, London WC2 0HR. Make cheques payable to TV Choice. The video is also available from Bookmarks, 1 Bloomsbury Street, London WC1B 3QE

The Socialist Workers Party is one of an international grouping of socialist organisations:

AUSTRALIA: International Socialists, PO Box A338, Sydney South

BRITAIN: Socialist Workers Party, PO Box 82, London E3

CANADA: International Socialists, PO Box 339, Station E, Toronto, Ontario M6H 4E3

CYPRUS: Ergatiki Demokratia, PO Box 7280, Nicosia

DENMARK: Internationale Socialister, Postboks 642, 2200 København N

GREECE: Sosialistiko Ergatiko Komma, c/o Workers Solidarity, PO Box 8161, Athens 100 10

HOLLAND: Internationale Socialisten, PO Box 92052, 1090 AA Amsterdam

IRELAND: Socialist Workers Party, PO Box 1648, Dublin 8

NEW ZEALAND:
Socialist Workers Organization, PO Box 8851, Auckland

NORWAY: Internasjonale Socialisterr, Postboks 5370, Majorstua, 0304 Oslo 3

POLAND: Solidarność Socjalistyczna, PO Box 12, 01-900 Warszawa 118

SOUTH AFRICA:
Socialist Workers Organisation, PO Box 18530, Hillbrow 2038, Johannesberg

SPAIN: Socialismo Internacional, Apartado 563, 08080, Barcelona

UNITED STATES:
International Socialist Organisation, PO Box 16085, Chicago, Illinois 60616

ZIMBABWE:
International Socialist Organisation, PO Box 6758, Harare

The following issues of *International Socialism* (second series) are available price £3 (including postage) from IS Journal, PO Box 82, London E3 3LH. *International Socialism* 2:58 and 2:65 are available on cassette from the Royal National Institute for the Blind (Peterborough Library Unit). Phone 01733 370777.

International Socialism 2:77 Autumn 1997
Audrey Farrell: Addicted to profit—capitalism and drugs ★ Mike Gonzalez: The resurrections of Che Guevara ★ Sam Ashman: India: imperialism, partition and resistance ★ Henry Maitles: Never Again! ★ John Baxter: The return of political science ★ Dave Renton: Past its peak★

International Socialism 2:76 Autumn 1997
Mike Haynes: Was there a parliamentary alternative in 1917? ★ Megan Trudell: Prelude to revolution: class consciousness and the First World War ★ Judy Cox: A light in the darkness ★ Pete Glatter: Victor Serge: writing for the future ★ Gill Hubbard: A guide to action ★ Chris Bambery: Review article: Labour's history of hope and despair ★

International Socialism 2:75 Summer 1997
John Rees: The class struggle under New Labour ★ Alex Callinicos: Europe: the mounting crisis ★ Lance Selfa: Mexico after the Zapatista uprising ★ William Keach: Rise like lions? Shelley and the revolutionary left ★ Judy Cox: What state are we really in? ★ John Parrington: In perspective: Valentin Voloshinov ★

International Socialism 2:74 Spring 1997
Colin Sparks: Tories, Labour and the crisis in education ★ Colin Wilson: The politics of information technology ★ Mike Gonzalez: No more heroes: Nicaragua 1996 ★ Christopher Hill: Tulmults and commotions: turning the world upside down ★ Peter Morgan: Capitalism without frontiers? ★ Alex Callinicos: Minds, machines and evolution ★ Anthony Arnove: In perspective: Noam Chomsky★

International Socialism 2:73 Winter 1996
Chris Harman: Globalisation: a critique of a new orthodoxy ★ Chris Bambery: Marxism and sport ★ John Parrington: Computers and consciousness: a reply to Alex Callinicos ★ Joe Faith: Dennett, materialism and empiricism ★ Megan Trudell: Who made the American Revolution? ★ Mark O'Brien: The class conflicts which shaped British history ★ John Newsinger: From class war to Cold War ★ Alex Callinicos: The state in debate ★ Charlie Kimber: Review article: coming to terms with barbarism in Rwanda in Burundi★

International Socialism 2:72 Autumn 1996
Alex Callinicos: Betrayal and discontent: Labour under Blair ★ Sue Cockerill and Colin Sparks: Japan in crisis ★ Richard Levins: When science fails us ★ Ian Birchall: The Babeuf bicentenary: conspiracy or revolutionary party? ★ Brian Manning: A voice for the poor ★ Paul O'Flinn: From the kingdom of necessity to the kingdom of freedom: Morris's *News from Nowhere* ★ Clare Fermont: Bookwatch: Palestine and the Middle East 'peace process'★

International Socialism 2:71 Summer 1996
Chris Harman: The crisis of bourgeois economics ★ Hassan Mahamdallie: William Morris and revolutionary Marxism ★ Alex Callinicos: Darwin, materialism and revolution ★ Chris Nineham: Raymond Williams: revitalising the left? ★ Paul Foot: A passionate prophet of liberation ★ Gill Hubbard: Why has feminism failed women? ★ Lee Sustar: Bookwatch: fighting to unite black and white★

International Socialism 2:70 Spring 1996
Alex Callinicos: South Africa after apartheid ★ Chris Harman: France's hot December ★ Brian Richardson: The making of a revolutionary ★ Gareth Jenkins: Why Lucky Jim turned right—an obituary of Kingsley Amis ★ Mark O'Brien: The bloody birth of capitalism ★ Lee Humber: Studies in revolution ★ Adrian Budd: A new life for Lenin ★ Martin Smith: Bookwatch: the General Strike★

International Socialism 2:69 Winter 1995
Lindsey German: The Balkan war: can there be peace? ★ Duncan Blackie: The left and the Balkan war ★ Nicolai Gentchev: The myth of welfare dependency ★ Judy Cox: Wealth, poverty and class in Britain today ★ Peter Morgan: Trade unions and strikes ★ Julie Waterson: The party at its peak ★ Megan Trudell: Living to some purpose ★ Nick Howard: The rise and fall of socialism in one city ★ Andy Durgan: Bookwatch: Civil war and revolution in Spain ★

International Socialism 2:68 Autumn 1995
Ruth Brown: Racism and immigration in Britain ★ John Molyneux: Is Marxism deterministic? ★ Stuart Hood: News from nowhere? ★ Lee Sustar: Communism in the heart of the beast ★ Peter Linebaugh: To the teeth and forehead of our faults ★ George Paizis: Back to the future ★ Phil Marshall: The children of stalinism ★ Paul D'Amato: Bookwatch: 100 years of cinema ★

International Socialism 2:67 Summer 1995
Paul Foot: When will the Blair bubble burst? ★ Chris Harman: From Bernstein to Blair—100 years of revisionism ★ Chris Bambery: Was the Second World War a war for democracy? ★ Alex Callinicos: Hope against the Holocaust ★Chris Nineham: Is the media all powerful? ★ Peter Morgan: How the West was won ★ Charlie Hore: Bookwatch: China since Mao ★

International Socialism 2:66 Spring 1995
Dave Crouch: The crisis in Russia and the rise of the right ★ Phil Gasper: Cruel and unusual punishment: the politics of crime in the United States ★ Alex Callinicos: Backwards to liberalism ★ John Newsinger: Matewan: film and working class struggle ★ John Rees: The light and the dark ★ Judy Cox: How to make the Tories disappear ★ Charlie Hore: Jazz: a reply to the critics ★ Pat Riordan: Bookwatch: Ireland ★

International Socialism 2:65 Special issue
Lindsey German: Frederick Engels: life of a revolutionary ★ John Rees: Engels' Marxism ★ Chris Harman: Engels and the origins of human society ★ Paul McGarr: Engels and natural science ★

International Socialism 2:64 Autumn 1994
Chris Harman: The prophet and the proletariat ★ Kieran Allen: What is changing in Ireland ★ Mike Haynes: The wrong road on Russia ★ Rob Ferguson: Hero and villain ★ Jane Elderton: Suffragette style ★ Chris Nineham: Two faces of modernism ★ Mike Hobart, Dave Harker and Matt Kelly: Three replies to 'Jazz—a people's music?' ★ Charlie Kimber: Bookwatch: South Africa—the struggle continues ★

International Socialism 2:63 Summer 1994
Alex Callinicos: Crisis and class struggle in Europe today ★ Duncan Blackie: The United Nations and the politics of imperialism ★ Brian Manning: The English Revolution and the transition from feudalism to capitalism ★ Lee Sustar: The roots of multi-racial labour unity in the United States ★ Peter Linebaugh: Days of villainy: a reply to two critics ★ Dave Sherry: Trotsky's last, greatest struggle ★ Peter Morgan: Geronimo and the end of the Indian wars ★ Dave Beecham: Ignazio Silone and *Fontamara* ★ Chris Bambery: Bookwatch: understanding fascism ★

International Socialism 2:62 Spring 1994
Sharon Smith: Mistaken identity—or can identity politics liberate the oppressed? ★ Iain Ferguson: Containing the crisis—crime and the Tories ★ John Newsinger: Orwell and the Spanish Revolution ★ Chris Harman: Change at the first millenium ★ Adrian Budd: Nation and empire—Labour's foreign policy 1945-51 ★ Gareth Jenkins: Novel questions ★ Judy Cox: Blake's revolution ★ Derek Howl: Bookwatch: the Russian Revolution ★

International Socialism 2:61 Winter 1994
Lindsey German: Before the flood? ★ John Molyneux: The 'politically correct' controversy ★ David McNally: E P Thompson—class struggle and historical materialism ★ Charlie Hore: Jazz—a people's music ★ Donny Gluckstein: Revolution and the challenge of labour ★ Charlie Kimber: Bookwatch: the Labour Party in decline ★

International Socialism 2:59 Summer 1993
Ann Rogers: Back to the workhouse ★ Kevin Corr and Andy Brown: The labour aristocracy and the roots of reformism ★ Brian Manning: God, Hill and Marx ★ Henry Maitles: Cutting the wire: a criticial appraisal of Primo Levi ★ Hazel Croft: Bookwatch: women and work ★

International Socialism 2:58 Spring 1993
Chris Harman: Where is capitalism going? (part one) ★ Ruth Brown and Peter Morgan: Politics and the class struggle today: a roundtable discussion ★ Richard Greeman: The return of Comrade Tulayev: Victor Serge and the tragic vision of Stalinism ★ Norah Carlin: A new English revolution ★ John Charlton: Building a new world ★ Colin Barker: A reply to Dave McNally ★

International Socialism 2:56 Autumn 1992
Chris Harman: The Return of the National Question ★ Dave Treece: Why the Earth Summit failed ★ Mike Gonzalez: Can Castro survive? ★ Lee Humber and John Rees: The good old cause—an interview with Christopher Hill ★ Ernest Mandel: The Impasse of Schematic Dogmatism ★

International Socialism 2:55 Summer 1992
Alex Callinicos: Race and class ★ Lee Sustar: Racism and class struggle in the American Civil War era ★ Lindsey German and Peter Morgan: Prospects for socialists—an interview with Tony Cliff ★ Robert Service: Did Lenin lead to Stalin? ★ Samuel Farber: In defence of democratic revolutionary socialism ★ David Finkel: Defending 'October' or sectarian dogmatism? ★ Robin Blackburn: Reply to John Rees ★ John Rees: Dedicated followers of fashion ★ Colin Barker: In praise of custom ★ Sheila McGregor: Revolutionary witness ★

International Socialism 2:54 Spring 1992
Sharon Smith: Twilight of the American dream ★ Mike Haynes: Class and crisis—the transition in eastern Europe ★ Costas Kossis: A miracle without end? Japanese capitalism and the world economy ★ Alex Callinicos: Capitalism and the state system: A reply to Nigel Harris ★ Steven Rose: Do animals have rights? ★ John Charlton: Crime and class in the 18th century ★ John Rees: Revolution, reform and working class culture ★ Chris Harman: Blood simple ★

International Socialism 2:51 Summer 1991
Chris Harman: The state and capitalism today ★ Alex Callinicos: The end of nationalism? ★ Sharon Smith: Feminists for a strong state? ★ Colin Sparks and Sue Cockerill: Goodbye to the Swedish miracle ★ Simon Phillips: The South African Communist Party and the South African working class ★ John Brown: Class conflict and the crisis of feudalism ★

International Socialism 2:49 Winter 1990
Chris Bambery: The decline of the Western Communist Parties ★ Ernest Mandel: A theory which has not withstood the test of time ★ Chris Harman: Criticism which does not withstand the test of logic ★ Derek Howl: The law of value In the USSR ★ Terry Eagleton: Shakespeare and the class struggle ★ Lionel Sims: Rape and pre-state societies ★ Sheila McGregor: A reply to Lionel Sims ★

International Socialism 2:48 Autumn 1990
Lindsey German: The last days of Thatcher ★ John Rees: The new imperialism ★ Neil Davidson and Donny Gluckstein: Nationalism and the class struggle in Scotland ★ Paul McGarr: Order out of chaos ★

International Socialism 2:46 Winter 1989
Chris Harman: The storm breaks ★ Alex Callinicos: Can South Africa be reformed? ★ John Saville: Britain, the Marshall Plan and the Cold War ★ Sue Clegg: Against the stream ★ John Rees: The rising bourgeoisie ★

International Socialism 2:44 Autumn 1989
Charlie Hore: China: Tiananmen Square and after ★ Sue Clegg: Thatcher and the welfare state ★ John Molyneux: *Animal Farm* revisited ★ David Finkel: After Arias, is the revolution over? ★ John Rose: Jews in Poland ★

International Socialism 2:42 Spring 1989
Chris Harman: The myth of market socialism ★ Norah Carlin: Roots of gay oppression ★ Duncan Blackie: Revolution in science ★ International Socialism Index ★

International Socialism 2:41 Winter 1988
Polish socialists speak out: Solidarity at the Crossroads ★ Mike Haynes: Nightmares of the market ★ Jack Robertson: Socialists and the unions ★ Andy Strouthous: Are the unions in decline? ★ Richard Bradbury: What is Post-Structuralism? ★ Colin Sparks: George Bernard Shaw ★

International Socialism 2:39 Summer 1988
Chris Harman and Andy Zebrowski: Glasnost, before the storm ★ Chanie Rosenberg: Labour and the fight against fascism ★ Mike Gonzalez: Central America after the Peace Plan ★ Ian Birchall: Raymond Williams ★ Alex Callinicos: Reply to John Rees ★

International Socialism 2:35 Summer 1987
Pete Green: Capitalism and the Thatcher years ★ Alex Callinicos: Imperialism, capitalism and the state today ★ Ian Birchall: Five years of *New Socialist* ★ Callinicos and Wood debate 'Looking for alternatives to reformism' ★ David Widgery replies on 'Beating Time' ★

International Socialism 2:30 Autumn 1985
Gareth Jenkins: Where is the Labour Party heading? ★ David McNally: Debt, inflation and the rate of profit ★ Ian Birchall: The terminal crisis in the British Communist Party ★ replies on Women's oppression and *Marxism Today* ★

International Socialism 2:29 Summer 1985
Special issue on the class struggle and the left in the aftermath of the miners' defeat ★ Tony Cliff: Patterns of mass strike ★ Chris Harman: 1984 and the shape of things to come ★ Alex Callinicos: The politics of *Marxism Today* ★

International Socialism 2:26 Spring 1985
Pete Green: Contradictions of the American boom ★ Colin Sparks: Labour and imperialism ★ Chris Bambery: Marx and Engels and the unions ★ Sue Cockerill: The municipal road to socialism ★ Norah Carlin: Is the family part of the superstructure? ★ Kieran Allen: James Connolly and the 1916 rebellion ★

International Socialism 2:25 Autumn 1984
John Newsinger: Jim Larkin, Syndicalism and the 1913 Dublin Lockout ★ Pete Binns: Revolution and state capitalism in the Third World ★ Colin Sparks: Towards a police state? ★ Dave Lyddon: Demystifying the downturn ★ John Molyneux: Do working class men benefit from women's oppression? ★

International Socialism 2:18 Winter 1983
Donny Gluckstein: Workers' councils in Western Europe ★ Jane Ure Smith: The early Communist press in Britain ★ John Newsinger: The Bolivian Revolution ★ Andy Durgan: Largo Caballero and Spanish socialism ★ M Barker and A Beezer: Scarman and the language of racism ★

International Socialism 2:14 Winter 1981
Chris Harman: The riots of 1981 ★ Dave Beecham: Class struggle under the Tories ★ Tony Cliff: Alexandra Kollontai ★ L James and A Paczuska: Socialism needs feminism ★ reply to Cliff on Zetkin ★ Feminists In the labour movement ★

International Socialism 2:13 Summer 1981
Chris Harman: The crisis last time ★ Tony Cliff: Clara Zetkin ★ Ian Birchall: Left Social Democracy In the French Popular Front ★ Pete Green: Alternative Economic Strategy ★ Tim Potter: The death of Eurocommunism ★